1995

# The Phoenix Poets

Series Editor: Burton Hatlen
Assistant Editor: Sylvester Pollet

Voices of the Lady: Collected Poems

Stuart Z. Perkoff

# VOICES OF THE LADY: COLLECTED POEMS

Edited and with an Introduction by Gerald T. Perkoff, M.D.
Preface by Robert Creeley

*Orono, Maine*
The National Poetry Foundation
1998

# ACKNOWLEDGEMENTS

Some of these poems were previously published in the following books: *The Suicide Room*, Karlsruhe: Jonathan Williams, 1956; *Eat the Earth*, Denver: Black Ace, 1971; *Kowboy Pomes*, Golden, Colorado: The Groupier Press, 1973; *Alphabet*, Los Angeles and Fairfax: Red Hill Press, 1973; *Only Just Above the Ground*, special issue #28 of *The Smith*, edited by Harry Smith, 1973; *How It Is, Doing What I Do*, Black Ace Books, edited by Tony Scibella, 1976; *Visions for the Tribe*, Black Ace/Temple of Man, *Bowery* 25, 1976; and *Love Is the Silence: Poems 1948-1974*, edited by Paul Vangelisti, Los Angeles and Fairfax: Red Hill Press, 1975.

Published by The National Poetry Foundation
University of Maine, Orono, Maine 04469-5752

Printed by Cushing-Malloy, Inc.
Ann Arbor, Michigan 48107

Distributed by
University Press of New England
Hanover and London

Library of Congress Number: 97-69918
ISBN 0-943373-49-2 (cloth)
ISBN 0-943373-48-4 (paper)

The publication of this book was made possible in part
by a grant from the Stephen and Tabitha King Foundation

*Dedicated to Stuart's children*
*Sasha, Ben, Rachel, and Eva*

# CONTENTS

# FOR STUART

Stuart Z. Perkoff stays a vivid presence despite all the years now passed since our first meeting in the pages of Cid Corman's *Origin 2*. Charles Olson's admiring letter of July 23, 1951, gives some sense of the impact Perkoff's two poems in that issue had made.

stuart perkoff:
                         i have just been telling creeley how very moved
i was last night to find you there (origin 2) with us

                                        that those
two poems of yrs belong with us, and are something neither of us,
or anyone else, can visit as you can such another hell

                                        that you
move me as the clearest speaking of such things i have heard in
this half century of the false forwarding of like cause . . .

I marked this first in a poem in RESISTANCE about, a year ago,
how, your fineness of ear and touch makes it possible to
reintroduce materials that so many others have torpedoed, and kept
torpedoing, since the days of—in our language, I'd say, Dickens . . .

What Olson then so respected was Perkoff's ability to take on the scale and fact of social despair and make of it a statement specific to what it was literally, not the usual conversion to charitable understanding or distancing social judgment. He had no intent to say more or less than what he was moved to say, and no pretension ever in any of it.

When we did first meet in person, toward the end of the fifties, it was at a reading he gave with Bruce Boyd for San Francisco State's Poetry Center, at the downtown venue as I recall. His mother Ann was with him and certainly was moved and proud that day. What I most remember is Stu's intense insistence on the seemingly simple fact that one must work with what ways of speech and circumstance one had been given. *If your sound is a drone, then drone it*—make that drone the most penetrating, particular sound possible. His own voice was deep, a solid bass, lovely! Seeing this small, paradoxically sturdy person with his ample recognition of others and his generous humor always, it was somehow like unexpectedly finding a daytime Santa Claus (except his beard was coal black) who worked all the seasons straight through. He was instantly good news and stayed so, despite all the bleak wear and tear of the life that followed.

Los Angeles at that time seemed light years away from San Francisco. The painters appeared to have what handle on the action artists there could get—except for jazz, which had its own company. I think of the painter John Altoon as a real part of that time and place. The Scot Alex Trocchi was also there for awhile. Then there was Stu's fellow poet Saul White. A few others no doubt as a book like Lawrence Lipton's *The Holy Barbarians* would tell. But I was always a long way away, first in New Mexico and then Buffalo, and what chance we did have to talk came with the distractions of my being on the road with work to do. Whenever he could, Stu would be there, sometimes comfortably heavy and relaxed, at others almost a ghost, frail, thin, whispering, but always warm, particular, clear in his own mind and in what he saw and spoke of as the world. I never thought of him as a victim or as someone led astray by evil companions. He certainly had no wish to get addicted to heroin or anything else, but given he was, he lived with it—not heroically, not evasively, just factually. It was part of himself and he took it therefore as real.

Bobbie Louise Hawkins says that Stuart Perkoff was the only one she knew who could use the common street talk, the then hip phrasing, in a way that felt undramatic, natural, not just an attempt to be like some other side of life or person. There was no sense of trying it on, slumming, etc. It was part and parcel with the same ability Charles Olson had so valued, the particular genius that could enter and take place wherever it found itself. I don't know what one thinks a prison is or what it's like to spend as much time as he did locked up but there as well he managed to stay real, simply so, and kept, in Pound's significant phrase, "his mind entire." He told of taking acid in situations that would terrify me, for instance, a jail cell in Terminal Island. How could he manage "space" in such compacted circumstance? Integrity has to mean much more humanly than the fact of keeping all the parts together. It's both inside and out, what one is and also takes as what one is, all at the same time. It doesn't have a necessary moral. Like it or not, being alive finds its own way to live of necessity.

My other senses of Stuart come mostly from his younger brother Simon, who was a good friend in New Mexico, a fledgling piano player then working with another old friend and poet, Max Finstein. It was Si who got for me fugitive tapes of Bud Powell all those years ago, which I remember then playing for

Allen van Buskirk, friend of David Rattray, both students at Dartmouth where we'd gone on invitation of Jack Hirschman, who had his first teaching job there, and his wife Ruth explodes at my attention to this student, so we leave sans my reading at all. Small world! Rattray's *How I Became One of the Invisible* would have delighted Stuart. Writing, wherever, whenever, is such presence as that book works to locate, and back of all the critical attempts at literary groupings and significant objectifying of accomplishments is that enduring company, maintaining as it can—like Jack Spicer's in San Francisco, or John Wieners and his friends in Boston. For poets Stuart was LA's heart.

Sasha Perkoff, Stuart's son, would be a whole other story. He knew the respect friends had for his father but he must also have seen how finally useless we were to make anything different. He was already a man-boy when not much more than fifteen or sixteen. I recall seeing him in a San Francisco bar with a friend, another boy two years older, both black with coal dust from having come up to the city on a freight they'd hopped, and the third friend with them missed and went under the wheels as they kept on moving. Hardly apt for a sixteen year old to witness and deal with, but this one had and was taking care of the other, still in shock. He was much like Stuart, same voice and beard, a bit bigger, more silent. He possessed an adamant integrity, a fierce, shy hope and a kid's deter- mined cockiness. Stuart was proud of him but he could not give him a place to grow up in, simply his own was endlessly self-destructing.

Last real times with Stuart were in the early seventies when he, his wife and their family had moved north to live in Mill Valley after he had come out of jail. He worked for the clothing manufacturer, Alvin Duskin, known to the San Francisco community as a liberal with practiced good intentions, such as the hir- ing of ex-cons. But Stuart, more knowledgeable, said he was not at all easy to work for, and the reason he provided such employment was that people in that situation came cheap and didn't complain for fear of breaking parole. As ever, it made useful sense to know what one was talking about.

Thinking now of all the poems he did get written, and of what he might have done otherwise had his life been a little less brutal, he early made the point that has to stick. *You do what you can do with what you get.* Poets don't invent the world. They live in it. Stu Perkoff never let go.

—Robert Creeley
Boulder, Colorado
June 7, 1997

13

# INTRODUCTION

This collection of the poems of Stuart Z. Perkoff represents a voyage of discovery and learning for me, his older brother. Stuart was a classic California poet during and after the Beat period in Venice, California, from the 1950s on, and as such his writings deserve attention and collection. One book which focuses on Stuart and his fellows in Venice[1] as well as an extensive biographical analysis[2] already have appeared. Interest in this period in American letters grows steadily.

My memories of Stuart are not those of a rebel poet. Instead they consist of a series of snapshots of a brilliant, charismatic, iconoclastic comet, one who shot through the early part of my family life only to disappear into a world I wished to avoid. My knowledge of him is, therefore, incomplete and inconsistent. In the latter part of his life, I grew closer to him once again. Since his death, my role in our family has been that of caretaker of the elderly and then older brother and uncle, a friend to Stuart's children. Almost daily, I learn more about this brother, a brilliant and much loved man, who poured out his heart and pain on paper in carefully crafted poems and voluminous journals which tell of his life and thoughts, fears and aspirations. I have been and am learning about Stuart through these evidences of himself.

My own memories of Stuart in his early years, of course, are different from recollections others may have of him. He was four years younger than I, but we spent a great deal of time together as children. We always walked to school together—I leading the way, he complaining that I was going too fast. I can see us now in plus-four knickers, walking rapidly along Hamilton Avenue in St. Louis, past business and quiet residential streets, past the show window of a local furniture mover which displayed a famous but gory beer company painting of the scalping of Custer's men at Little Big Horn, alternately stopping to stare and hurrying by to avoid the fright the painting induced in us both. In the summer we frequently played in a washtub under a portable, outdoor shower to stay cool.

[1] Maynard, John Arthur. *The Beat Generation in Southern California.* New Brunswick, NJ: Rutgers UP, 1991.
[2] Griffiths, David B. "On the Life and Poetry of Stuart Zane Perkoff (1930-1974)." *The Abiko Quarterly* 7.15 (Fall 1995): 287-348. Abiko-shik, Chiba-kan 270-11, Japan.

This was the only access we had to a "swimming pool" in those days. I think of that period as typical of older brother/younger brother times, with a mixture of pride and exasperation on my part and a memory of big brother worship and aggravation on his. Even in retrospect, there was little in Stuart's relationships with me or with others that was obviously different or unusual.

Things changed rapidly as we grew older. Stuart was a rebel from his early years on, running away from home for some unknown reason as early as age nine. He became interested in politics, and as some of his poems describe, frequented anarchist/leftist slum areas of St. Louis while he was in his mid-teens. Withal, he was a fine student, active and successful in drama at Clayton High School, and then and thereafter always attractive to women. Years later, when my family and I returned to Clayton, Missouri, to live during my own children's school years, women would seek out my wife and me at PTA meetings and other functions to ask if we were related to Stuart and to tell us how much they had always loved him.

His middle and later years were less well known to me. He was an early and active member of the beat generation, a leader in the Venice, California, group of poets and musicians who followed in the paths of Ginsberg, Patchen, and Kerouac. With them he rejected material things, standard relationships, and often, it seemed, society at large. He and his friends used drugs heavily, and lived an alternative life style I instinctively rejected. Our contacts then were brief, irregular, and widely separated. Only later, when he was in prison for dealing drugs, did I re-establish regular contact and learn again to know him well. He stopped using drugs while he was in prison, and, to my knowledge, only used them intermittently when he was released. Stuart always said it was easier to get drugs—any drugs—in prison than on the street, so his reduced use surely was voluntary. This made it particularly poignant during his final illness with metastatic lung cancer, when he was given morphine to control his pain. He commented wryly, "They've made me a junkie again." He died just before his forty-fourth birthday.

These poems are important to me personally, and as I read and transcribe them, I learn more and more of their importance to others. This was an interesting and vital man with much to say about the fears, angers, and yes, the angst of the young people of his time. For both personal and literary reasons, then, I feel impelled to make whatever parts of them I can available to others to read for their intrinsic value, even as they serve me as a reintroduction to a brother I "knew not well."

The organization of what follows is simple. The collection begins with five collections of poetry that Stuart prepared for publication during his lifetime, printed in the order of publication. These are followed by three collections edited by friends of Stuart after his death, omitting only poems included in earlier collections. These collections are followed by a group of poems published in a variety of little magazines and broadsides that sprang up in the beat culture of the fifties and sixties. These poems are arranged chronologically, in order of publication. Then comes a book-length but unpublished group of poems called *The Venice Poems*, and a large number of previously unpublished poems by Stuart, arranged in three groups by the decades in which they were written. It is almost certain that there are more poems that I have not found. It was common for Stuart to give poems to friends, and only some, but certainly not all of them, have now been given to me. Equally certainly, poems published in some short-lived broadsides did not survive their early years.

A word about the methods I used to place the unpublished poems in the order in which they appear here. Those unpublished poems which are dated are placed by that date. When dates were not noted on the original poem, Stuart's journals were searched and poems found there were dated according to the period in which the most complete version was found. For those poems not located in the journals, typescripts of poems of unknown dates were compared with those with known dates. Stuart used several different typewriters and typescripts over the years, and there are dated poems in each typescript. It was possible to place a number of poems in the time period of a particular typescript with some assurance that the dating was correct. This, plus some period-specific content (i.e., the Viet Nam War, prison) makes me reasonably certain of the dates of most of the poems presented here.

In editing these poems, I have silently corrected some obvious typos, but I have tried to preserve Stuart's sometimes idiosyncratic spelling and typography. Stuart left many of his poems untitled. Such poems are here labelled *Untitled*. The italics are intended to indicate that these labels have been added by the editor.

I also should comment about my choice of a title for this volume. Stuart believed strongly that his poems originated not with him, but with his muse, the Lady. He viewed himself as the physical and emotional vehicle she used to record her words. There are poems to the Lady scattered throughout this work, and all of them can be considered "Voices of the Lady."

As is always the case, many people have helped me with this work. Especially helpful were the librarians of the Division of Special Collections at the University of California at Los Angeles, especially Ms. Ann Cager, where the originals of all of Stuart's journals and existing copies of most of his works are stored. In addition, Rachel Perkoff Di Paola, Stuart's daughter, and his friends Susan Stearns, Joan Martin, Tony Scibella, Frank Rios, and Philomene Long contributed poems and sound advice. Allen Ginsberg and Beverly Jarrett were especially helpful in guiding my search for a publisher. I am deeply indebted to Robert Creeley for agreeing to prepare his personal reminiscences of Stuart for this volume. I also wish to thank the staff of the National Poetry Foundation, especially Burton Hatlen, Jill Randall, Sylvester Pollet, and Mark Melnicove, who labored heroically to transform a pile of manuscript into a coherent book.

There are in this collection beautiful poems, poems which depict an ugly world and troubled time of life, and poems which are difficult to understand. But together they tell a remarkable story of a brilliant mind cut short by fatal illness. To the extent that people leave behind evidence of themselves that represents their immortality, these poems are Stuart's living legacy of ideas and thoughts to us all.

—Gerald T. Perkoff, M.D.

*The Suicide Room* (1956)

## TO BE READ ON FESTIVAL DAYS

The basket is wrapped in gay
bright colors, with ribbons woven

within itself. A pattern of love
covers its mouth, inviting touch

and beckoning to the uninterested
onlooker.

When opened, a hard stream of
pain spurts out

to frighten little children.


## THREE EPIGRAMS

1.

Death lives near the spring morning.
In the East, the sound of guns
quiets birds. Here lovers dream
in vain of soft silent days.


2. FOR FRIENDS LEAVING

This black undersoul of terror
(our world) destroys
the quick fragile loves. One now
shatters. Only the brilliant splinters
are left in the heart, and tears.

3.

Those who wake with innocence
in the morning,
bed down at night with death
upon their tongues.


THE PLAYGROUND


Lined up against the wall in twos
the children stand.
And raise their hands in time.
Small gods beat numbers from their
throats, and boys
and girls, in separate lines
raise their hands and lower them,
in time.

One stands
in a corner of the yard, throwing
a ball against the wall,
alone. The ball bounces to him:
thrown again, it flies off
towards the street.
In glaring light of sun and eyes
the ball rolls off,
out of sight.

Lined up against the wall, two lines
of children watch the ball roll
into the street, while tiny gods
beat numbers from their teachers' throats.

# THE WORD "THEE"

Thee. Say the word. Thee.
This is a lost word. Hear
it echo off the walls of
mind, alone, seeking, alone.

Say it loudly. Whisper it.
Kiss it. Turn it in your hands.
Thee. What is this word?
Is it a machine? A gun trigger?
Is it a weapon, new and clean?
Can this word be oiled, and shined?

Thee. Hear the word. Thee.
This poor lost word, shivering
in the cold rooms of our world.


# FOR B. L.

There is a wildness in the night when we meet, a rushing of fire
to water, a pounding of wave
upon wave, body upon body. Tooth to breast the beast of love emerges
from the heart, and attacks.

There is a hatred in the air as we dance over each other,
a laughter of knives,
flesh hardens, hands clench, nerves jut out strong and large, the
    whole embattled bodies meet and clash against each other,
split asunder and envelop
the blood and bone and hot breath of love. Agony is muffled,
withheld screams tear through the tightness of muscle,
claw and flesh strike.

There is a music in the night when we are together,
when the beast of love comes forth, and dances on the bodies
of the lovers.


## THE BLIND GIRL

Her mirror reflects the emptiness of
life's full turn. Her mirror is made

of black steel, shiny and sharp and new
with newness of never being used for evil.

Her weeping hands caress the breasts
which she feels protruding from her delicate chest.

Long silken fingers enter and return to
the holy nest of untouched love.

The holes in her head see all and nothing
in her world. Her world is made of soft

green things, and weeping hands, and tender
breasts, and furry small orgasms.

She does not even know her hair is black.


## THE SUICIDE ROOM

I have within the head a room of death:
brown walls (the death of spring), a vague breath of
seasmell, a ring of knives of every kind
circling a centered mat.

                         The failing lives
to be accompanied by flat drums,
dovecooing horns, plucked strings.
                         The supplicant comes,
he sits upon the mat. Attendants bring
paper and pen. He wills his philosophy
to the world and binds his eyes. And blind he dies.

This is the room I go to when my mind
extends no further than its hidden doom.
I weld the music and the knives into
a power over deaths.

                         I leave the dead
within this room when I have held power
for long enough to go beyond the point
beyond which one cannot possibly go.

## FLOWERS FOR LUIS BUÑUEL

What is the word for 'death'
in French? What word triggers
laughter at slit eyes and guttered
cripples?
                 What is the word for
the language of the eye, the montage of
blood?

                 Buñuel, Buñuel,
the musicians in the building play no tune
comparable to the whirring lens
of hideous glare of light and blood.
The knives and dwarfs and round firm tits
say death in French for a language too
strong to hold in the gut.

Buñuel, Buñuel,
is the world? A place?
                    such dirty
coños and open flies! an unwiped ass
editing the noise of the city,
the wind an instrument of long black hair,
all the mothers dying.

Let us go to the cinema.
Let us go
            to the sinema.
Every rock depends for life upon
the spilling of blood, and torn flesh.
Every death creates a small quiver,
a hatred of mirrors.
                Who knew guilt
before this? The eye, the eye,
burning too steadily through the ugly night
in the theatre dark with the smells
of all our hatred. The cinema of
the slit, the wound, the crawling ants.
Buñuel, did you do it? Did you?
Have you built the handless queer,
the only sighted murderer? Have you
built them?

            Let the misshapen dance
around the rock. Only a priest can eat
this shit and not vomit. This is the
cross made of bones. Prayers? Never!

            Buñuel, Buñuel,
is the world? Did you?

# A TOKEN

"Why don't you"
           she said
"write poems any more

"to me?"
        and indeed
why not?

neatly trimmed and limned and lined
have been
wheelbarrows as well as passions

                a communication
                across the room
                of a marriage

"good morning darling
"is there coffee
"I'm late for work
"did the kids
                eat lunch?"
           Well,
        did they?

What would it include?
a shout down the years of our mutual
enclosure.
the symbols of the loaf of bread

and
the
sharp
      knife

read many different ways.

# SONG

*for Rudolph Crosswell*


I live with madmen,
and sing among their mirrored dreams.

If sometimes spoken are
such words,
               "what am I
           "doing here?",
                        I am reminded of
the deadly logic of all the mad.
Who protests his sanity? I do,
              yet,
              is this not another trick
the always hunted uses to
defy the rest?

I live among madmen, and sing
the mirror of their dreams.
I, mad, among
the living men, dream the
mirror of their songs.

Living, I sing madly dreaming,
mirroring among men.

## PANSIES

*—D. H. Lawrence titled one of his last books
of poems "Pansies," a deliberate corruption
of the French "Pensées."*

Pansies means thoughts, a book of quick sharp poems.
Or else it means young homosexuals, painted brittle
    blond colors for their lovers.
Didn't it use to mean a flower,
some sort of warm bright growing thing? I don't
even remember clearly what it looks like, but I always
       think of it
as having a face in the middle, and bright yellow
around itself, looking to the sun.

Well, the world changes around a flower, and now
in answer to its name the flower finds
a slender banned book,
and on the other hand the slender banned young men.
Book, flower, boys, all
with some sort of yellow around themselves,
looking for the sun.

## THE WIND

Last night it came, late, and swept
along between the houses, chilled in
the open windows.
        Outside
a tin can and a bottle rolled up and down
the rough street. They made a noise
like a horse-drawn wagon,
filled with junk and broken windows.

"I thought
"it was part of the music," she said.

There was only one star in the sky,
and a moon slice.
The world hung suspended from them
in the blackness,
                    suspended by strings
of bells and Chinese glass, swaying

and ringing
in the wild wind.


## THE CHESS PLAYERS AT THE BEACH


A child screamingly scatters pigeons
among the old men. Black and white
fly and settle.
                    The reality moves.
The abstract moves. The ancient language
(a fitting accompaniment) expends its
dying days above the boards.

From Canaan into history they have moved,
absorbing bits of life and words,
weaving them into their great dark world.
From behind walls, from shattered small houses
they arrive at this ocean to push the pieces,
playing at wars they have always kept within themselves.

Eternally cast out, they sit in the sun
touching community property,
slowly moving it within the limited space,
*as though it were theirs*!
                    Gloving their hands
with miracles, they try to transform loss

to gain, hatred to love.
                    During
the hours of daylight, beside the pigeoned child,
they seek again the holiness of the race.


## AT THE END OF THE UPRISING
*for Jackson Mac Low*


And thus blood.
Seldom flowing softly: in spurts
covering guns, spoiling aim.

And then the children screaming:
"Bread! Bread!" and the small
armies of women combing streets.

Grass still growing in
cracks between
            cement blocks,
no smoke, but fire and blood
covering guns, spoiling aim.

Tho the walls stand shabbily
the gangs of children
roam the meager streets,
and cry "Bread! Bread!"

This is the end of hate:
            the women cry
the buildings stand,
            the children scream
and blood covers the guns,
spoiling aim.

# SPRING

*after a painting by John Hultberg*

Walk out under the trees with me, and see
death covering the horizon like a thin piece of gauze,
the ground an open wound to
quicksand the soul, the patch of green a thinly disguised
tombstone, with name and date carefully
hidden, until upon close inspection it spells the world.

Walk out into the land with me,
warmly clothed against the chill brown sun,
and dance between these trees. Their arms thrust fearfully
to the sky, their mouths scream.
Surely, in the background, out of human sight, a gun
is trained on them, and now, as we stumble
through our clumsy dance,
on us as well.

Darling, walk out among the trees, upon the land.
Walk with me towards the deadly horizon,
for we are alone here. We are here alone.
Let us walk, and walk, and walk,
as the open wounded ground grasps raspingly
at our clumsy souls.

*Eat the Earth* (1971)

o morning star
o morning raging sea
or morning lite breaking in my eye
as the last fragments of nite cling to my tongue
& i try to spit prayers
into the swift air, real
& cold
cold inside my nose & head
cold & sharp, the air with the smash song rumble of the dancing
                                    waves
flowing fast frenetic foam poem
sounds
grey & white & wild &
unaware of my pain, my blood
unaware of my song, my needs, my love
pushing transparent fingers up, over the sand, over the banked
                                        wall
crash ringing boom bam sing song terror womb
announcing the new day

o hear my knees crack
as i kneel in broken prayer
hear the Lady's brite wings flick & flap
across the eye of the great sea
across the eye of the wet cold sand
across the eye of hard clear song stained air
that blows from nowhere to nowhere
carrying all songs, singing, sounds, breathing
carrying flight & dance, wing, fear, sudden ecstasy
                        of breath

from nowhere to nowhere
across the sand face of venice
from nowhere to nowhere
dancing the gliding gulls in the fluid air
from nowhere to nowhere
across my too human eyes

across my bleeding mouth
across my clumsy hands, & my
naked
desires


CONTINUED FROM LAST WEEK'S EPISODE

will our hero, blacked by flame, bent by fate, scraped,
slammed, battered, hysterical, catatonic, strong armed, red
white & blue blooded, chaste, obedient, disciplined, damned
pull himself out of the bloody herochopper perched on top of the
poet's mountain?

        will he return to the world in time
to save the merry maiden from the clutches of the
archly mustachioed, ultravillainous sharpcreased four
buttoned arrow shirt monster madison avenue copycatwriter?

        it is the end of the
episode:  chapter four.  the hero
trapped in a fiery pit, ringed with knives, shot by guns
spurned by his cheerleader happygomaltshop girl friend—
                        flash!
                                buck rogers, flash gordon & dr
fu manchu will meet in a triple ringed arena, where captain
midnite & jack armstrong, in a fight to the finish—

        o, the heroes die, the heroes die
the radio is turned off, & in the sloping attic room
the child that i was turns & writhes in his herofilled
dreams, terrified, as children are

                give a little love, win three for a
ten cent piece, throw the little bullshit at the lady
step right up & test yr arm aim or what have you
want you give you throw you bang!

    & as we look in on a little old ma
perkins & her four wheel drive chrome plated
rustproof fully american traveling commodious spacious
comfortable dignified aristocratic ultimately
economical whorehousemobile we find ma making
breakfast in the kitchen.  ma is not shy, but
fred breakfast is embarrassed to be discovered by
the television cameras while sucking ma perkins'
greyhaired wrinklemouthed cavernous cunt

ten years & three children
later, we find our hero
hanging by the neck dangling
outside the window
hoping someone will pull
him in & water him

## POEM IN MY THIRTIETH SUMMER

1.

i think others bleed to
feed my poems.  christ may have
chosen, these seldom
know.
        wounds / swallowed
into them, others
pain is what
i mean.

not to say no one
listens, that doesnt enter
it. ears & the tongue, the
breath, it is again
the flight of the bird, the whole
word. no.  as the

attention turns
in, so might anything.  the best
shown demands pity.


2.


i wont lick no sick
dont want to be leper-lover, dont want
to want it.

take yr hands off my
monster, he'll kill you, & i'll
laugh.  the chimp
knows, ask
him if i hate.  i do.  & maybe
dig to see that blood.
nothing will grow, nothing
meet,  no
touch.  i haven't choice.


3.


shd be obvious the birds
know what they have, laugh,
game.

can we know
& clumsy our loves to
each other?

the gull's morning is
real, up with the first lite, out
hungry, over the water, entering his
proper rhythm.  yet i say
love.  as tho to close
wounds, take blood taste from
the throat.
   the body knows.

let the animal take
over.  it is the single
voice, only, not
better or purer, not anything
but here.  now.  one man
saying one man's things

works clutter any street
no one tries to say
love
or touch
real
for good
reason

but what flows
my hand & draws blood, that
needs no sounding.
                              birds may
hurt with no
whimpers, but not men.  no.  i
cant do it.


4.

i move in
america, & still love
the tongue

surgeons were once
lowly, shops stank blood & piss.
who scrapes the bone of lie with dull & magic.
knife now
differs but slightly

        walk close
to the ground. sing
close to the music.  love

close to the body.  that's all
i can say.


5.

any hand in any
life
destroys.  the bird wing
tells me what i
am, that is to say, human.
                        the one
voice
is difficult enuf / here are
my own faces, here is
love.  unspeakable.  what but
the one man's
sound
        isnt?


*UNTITLED*


turned loose in the streets
we eat the earth itself in
search of visions

earth tastes like 50 billion years
earth tastes
like everything that ever died is
in yr mouth clot-
ting yr teeth filling & packing
the throat.  earth
tastes the tree that will
it tastes like grow
from the bellied earth we eat

when i began eating earth
i hoped i wd soon learn somehow
thru the taste, texture, consistency
of each mouthful /
                        somehow
know the
taste of the earth fleeing the sun, the
taste of the moon's rejection, the taste
of god's own hand moving aside the void
to thrust his own mouth
into the earth, to eat
the earth

hoped i cd devour, ingest, make
integral with my flesh
all the time of man & not man
cities, graves, blood
the goddess descending, the murderers of gods, the loves, the
                                                    water
everything
must be there it seemed logical i
hoped.  eating the earth
seeking vision

vision to vision, eating to mouth
out of earth grows flesh
& to the flesh earth eager returns
to fill the eyes & belly with its rich self
to send out feelers within, to
mate, sprout
begin to seed

sitting at the top of the venice scumball machine
disguised as a mechanical candy dandy handy andy poet opener
i can shift my eyes all around my pink candy shell
& i can smell the stink of the pink candy smell
hanging up on the brink of the pink candy hell
& i watch them putting on their disguises
with their shifty b-picture eyeses

sitting in the brite colored backache redeyed scumball latrine
i watch them stick their fing-
                                    ers ick-
                                        y into a
phony poem machine.
that's the scam.
waiting to be chewed in the great venice slam
waiting to be punched in my imitation nose
waiting to be hung from my prehensile toes

the scumball machine is gigantic
the huge money bellies are frantic
they keep putting pennies into the nickel slot
hoping to drop my pink candy head into their scumball pot

but we are
alert.  there are still a few tricks
at the disposal
of the secret six.

# SATURDAY AFTERNOONS IN THE 1930'S

to slip in while the usher is flashing his lite all thru the
theatre & one of yr buddies got caught he's beginning to cry & will
probably snitch. THEN TO WIN A PAIR OF ROLLER SKATES AT THE POPEYE CLUB
TICKET STUB #691-183. that same day. & even munching popcorn,
tho I dont know where it came from.

or how bob (curley) steele's hat never came off but after a fight
he'd run his never took those tite gloves off hand thru his hair.
long & greasy. i always thot he was wise to keep his hat on.

what do you call it? luck? or american magic? still, they
closed one summer for repairs right at chapter nine of a buck rogers
serial, & when they reopened in september they had a new serial en-
tirely. they wdnt let my brother & me in in short pants one time. also
once they threw me out for yelling too loudly for the hero.

to show all is not perfect.

but thru it all that hat stayed on that head: jump off an over-
hang, pull villain to the earth, bam! pow! the whole shot! roll in the
dust, hat on head. swim in rivers, hat never comes off.

there's something special abt that kind of luck
that kind of world
too pure to be magic, & senseless, like so much of america

at least he didnt sing

it never bothered me, that strange american belief in its own
purity. i was certainly not alone in my awareness that it was false.

flowers & revolutions grew in our ashpits. the adults of the
world dont know how close they came in 1936 to losing the whole thing.

43

to shoot up the town on payday
to not care that the leading lady is wearing false breasts
to kill for the privilege of dying with honor
to never lose
these the rewards of that luck

now it is easy to see america rotting at the core
easy to be insane, be in jail
be hurting,  crying

nobody has one of those hats any more, that dont come off.

   i dont know how it is with the kids now, maybe they dont
think such a hat is possible.  a head for such a hat. but they must
have some thing or structure they dream pure.

   even while we mocked, i know i wanted once to be worthy of such a
hat.  to run my tite gloved hands thru my hair.


## JUNK NURSERY RHYMES


1.


mother, may i go out to fix?
yes, my darling daughter
you may tie yr arm & punch yr vein
but fill the spike with water


2.


sing a sick a song dance
arm full of cry
20 grains of morphine
shot into yr eye

when the eye is open
the world begins to sing, & sting
so fix my lads, & lassies, too
for crying is the thing


3.

sick jack horner
stood on the corner
waiting to meet with the man
he stood thru the nite
& into the lite
for all i know there he still stands

poor jack


4.

o do you know the hungry monk?
the hungry monk?
the hungry monk?
o do you know the hungry monk, he lives
between yr shoulders

yes i know the hungry monk
the hungry monk
the hungry monk
yes i know the hungry monk
he lives between my shoulders


5.

junkie, junkie, where have you been?
trying to score, out in the scene.
junkie, junkie, did you score enuf?
if there was that much, it wdnt be stuff.

6.

to market, to market to cop half a gram
into my arm to find the spike jammed

all over town to borrow a gun
fixed under a street lite / o had lots of fun

risk & adventure / run out of breath
my special market sells wings of death


7.

there was a young poet who lived in a zoo
he listened / he was human
he did what he cd do

he hated the murder of his legs & arms
he insulted the monkey
so it brought him harm
it put him in jail / now he dreams of his need
while the monk runs the streets on a new hungry steed


8.

bleeding rotten
he stole the cotton
hoping he wd fly

he got busted for those marks
& wasnt even high

*UNTITLED*

the gulls move thru the air, as tho
there were no air, as tho
all were air, & weightlessness.

even on the ground, in awkward dress
as tho there were no ground, no air, as tho
all were ground & air.
they are slow.  they do not show
all to the people who are there.

they move thru the world, as tho
there were no world, as tho
all were world & air, as tho
all were ocean & fire.  they know
the futility of desire.
they move higher.

*UNTITLED*

o all prisoners, madmen, terrified jailers & wives
halt in yr day's destruction
to homage the Queen
hands wrapped around steel bars across blind eyes
windows to nowhere where the sunset is black
& the stars are shamed to blink their million universed
                              songs of lite

the swinging rocking gently maddened
bloody hands with nails torn
clutching at the dust of ageless pain
digging in the airless desert
for the sweet freshets of holy death

Lady, my ten fingers freeze in fright
Lady, my gut screams for yr love
Lady, my eyes havent the strength to stay open
& what they see when you are not my lens
is more than human eye can bear.  anywhere

o blood my arms with manna
smash my bones with love
tenderly my heart gently its sad wounds
ripped tongue of silent scream
torn lungs emptied of fetid air

the death i breathe is only what i can without hope
there is the road but my feet shrivel
the fat & holy pigeons mock my tears
my city lifts its claws & turns on me
the children ring me with signs & curses
all my demons tumble out my mouth

o fold my crumpled tongue into yr mouth
my darling, my darling
sew my gaping heart with yr strong fingers

       not that it matters to the pavement if my blood washes its grime
       the trees can drink the air which i cannot breathe
       the children's laughter will dance by my ruptured ear

is all this just to say i love you?
o i love you my Muse
my Muse
my Muse

# A COLLAGE FOR TRISTAN TZARA

broken the
broken the
wood iron coal steel
an art gallery that sells collages in which there is a collage
     with a photograph of an art gallery that sells
     collages like the quaker oats man torn from a
     newpaper

   *tzara i am building this collage*
   *of actual things because i no longer know*
   *what is a poem*
   *& because you are tristan tzara*

heroin, tzara
marijuana
dreams & fears in many colors, dont forget them

on my wall it says:

     wyatt earp
     john garfield
     dr fu manchu
     pooh the poet
     dr doolittle
     dashiell hammett
     the land of oz
     i j singer
     erich von stroheim
     charlie chan
     orson welles
     captain midnite
     the shadow
     ben turpin
     buñuel
     alex berkman
     the man who invented heroin
     charlie parker

thelonius sphere monk
henry fonda
raymond chandler
tennyson
yeats
eliot
charlie brown
johnnie mack brown
pound
john ford
wordsworth
sherlock holmes
jackson pollock
ma perkins
rembrandt
chaucer
raggedy ann
cocteau
dostoyevsky
edgar allen poe
michael gold
patchen
bob (curley) steele
robert creeley
kurt schwitters
    people i dig
    in no special order
    She knows them all
& it says:
    "remove the shoes which clothe yr feet, & you
    will find that the ground upon which you stand
    even now is holy ground."—buber


into the collage with them, tzara, along with
MAN COMMITS SUICIDE WHEN HE DISCOVERS
    WORD WILL NOT DESTROY
RIPPED RIPPED RIPPED ANYTHING CD HAVE BE A
    BABY'S FOOT
MAYBE OR ANGEL WING TEAR TORN SLASHED

along with /
                piles of bones
                theatre tickets

do you think you recognise this collage, tzara?
no.  it is the similarity of all chaos.

let me put me into the collage
tzara. let me put you in it
also.

    tzara, they are glueing us
down.  tzara, we are hanging in
a gallery.  tzara, a fat rich woman is buying
us.  for her house.

how's that,  eh,  tzara? never can tell
which way a collage
will go


## UNTITLED


almost every day frankie & tony & i
three stooge it down the beach into the world
on the sharp lookout for
poems & dope & love &
colors reflecting off the laughter

frankie, what junkbent nose did you use to smell out
my need as i walked on the warm
feet of high ocean birds doing fredmacmurray
                messerschmitts in the clean air
walking, praying to the muse for a poet to talk to
without
names mask dancing

without bullshit fencing
just real

ranked frank stumbling in black leather veins in the
false venice warmth
falling on his stone chipped head
imbedding shrapnels of scream
irrevocably into my ear. then, up, again, determined as
the nineteenth century, lurching, thrusting
naked arms toward the empty
eyes sewn tite against
the horror of his peppermint mouth
hey, frankie! banned brother under the
belly, under the table, under sharp
thread hung sword of
                              "they'll take us away
& feed our garbaged brains
to soldier killers addicted to poet blood"

hey! hipster of the delicate glass streets of junkiest bronx
coming in, kicking, sick, throw
man up yr
eyes, up yr soul
bleeding tears on pavement splotch
poet of sad junk, poet of needles
poet of running the sidewalk cracks
down the street in the head
with a sick heartbeat

    o moon, moon
    you go too soon
    like the bird across the face of
    the clock eye hand striking
    the needle from the hand while it's still in the arm


    moon, moon, where are you, moon?
    you were resting so soft in the charred, bent spoon

hey white faced moonchaser with black jacket poems
bursting their long hipster sideburns between yr
                              shoes squeezed
toes
fungoid paranoid o boid he cries yr woid
poems


the craziest newspaper boy ever horatio algered
running around with urgent messages
abt the escape of black & its dangerous
consequences
                    in news poems of slashing each other's
blood filled throats
any nite between the dark & the lite
don't tell no one.  ninety third floor.  bring this message
                                    to the door
& in thru the broken windows
of their cocks
great leaping acrobats of death
poem in & promptly begin to strangle their
                        bewildered handler
all the while jumping thru hoops of flame balancing
statesmen's secret corsets & indian clubs filled with bad junk


climbing into a continuous shifting vaudeville of babel high
from which they swing the gaunt-jawed
bronx boy with a noose-tite grip
his junk hoarse voice drowned
in rumpty tumpty rhythms of the blood-fat grave dancers


Hey frankie, tony, let's get high
& dream our verse & painting to the purest sin
huffle scuffle madman shuffle like streetcorner dancers
with kazoo & jug singing the people's secret jazzsins
they're heating the coins before they toss them, because
                                    it's sunday


but we'll pick them up from the mothermurdering sidewalk
& watch hate burning red death hot fires of steel & corrupt
sizzle out in our kisswet hands

o we're a lucky crew, a jolly crew
three mad men in a pot pod boat
crashing up & down in the sun's white throat
bouncing spindizzy downsaults off the storefronts' very
                                   disapproving eyes

hey! rally the secret six
to save the maidens
cop the stash
disappear in the rainbow to look

at the ocean from the very peak
of a venice dungheap made of torn poet stomachs

to explode onto the ocean front
another day in the newborn sun
three simple maniacs trying carefully not to step
on the ancient & most properly venerated
race of
cockroach
in honor of which hard backed longlived godwon single
                           minded  perpetual bug
the beautiful butt end of the marijuana of love
was named one day
somewhere, by someone who may have been
any of us
you, me, if
we cd we
wd

shooting morphine in san francisco
with the graceful gracious boston poet
protected by the oz book love
wrapped warm around the house
i thot of you, frankie & tony
i thot of bird, & running, of love &
i thot of venice.  i thot of
a lot of things
          what abt a world
where the streets are paved with true dreams?

mother, may i go out to fix?
yes my darling daughter
you may tie yr arm & punch yr vein
but fill the spike with water

mother, may we go out to poem?
only if you find it
circling around, under the ground
& come up, blind, behind it

frankie, you invented a new language because you can't
                                        read old ones
tony, you invented
a new language of silence
because you cant speak old lies
no words
serves you well

& who served you to me, on what golden love feast platter
which god banquet did i accidently sit down to, both of you, who
                                        are, after all
only human.  not much can be expected
from you.  or me

but we run along the edges of the dame's dice, dancing
with her own stacked deck she dealt us the sound
of that old steamboat horn saxophone blowing up
a river slave chained
black africa blowing harlem disaster up & down stairs, leaping
thru jagged glass on the vast expanse of new york roofness

hey, cry, riverhorn, cry!
pierced to the piano with funny needles
fucking a thousand dead whores & wives
hey, you, saxophone! how many
holes you got in yr
head, arms, metal neck, metal eyes
to let in the sun lite
from which great rockets of pain & sound
smash moonward, red with blood

dark cotton swabbed hands bellyweaveling out of back room
                              monster jails of the mind
tooting that true sound to our turned on ears
that old steam boat horn twisting
into electric neon bombs


& just think, tony
when we first met
our throats were so clogged we cd only make hurt
gurgles.  throatcut sounds.  my mouth was filled
to fat cheeks breaking
with the vomit of my own self rising.
yr throat i've often thot of as
welling full
with the silver tears of nameless children


y're almost as hard to poem
as my wife, harder than frankie, he dances in from the bronx
                    doing his yoga bit walking on upturned spikes
                    bare everythinged
dazzling yr sun fuzzy brain with his songs of incoherent ferris
                    wheel dizzy
picking yr pocket by special remote control techniques
                    developed
                    in a certain better remain anonymous bronx cellar
& impossible to resist
                    but closeness breeds a kind of terrified awe


reality is so
                    now
it strikes my audacious fingers dumb & impertinent
reaching up the glass poems to
the brite orange & black jellybeans of love
when the storekeeper isnt looking


did we discover god together on a dark
pillhead working thru nite
throwing paints at each other
5 points for yellow 3 points for green
blue dont cost nothing it's just sky blood

                    each day i notice
we get thinner. fleshing our faces down, seeking the skull

it's scary to fall into
a great thick explosion painting, & not panic, learn to
breathe thru the fingers, & to smash
our sick minds

what did we think we were doing driving naked & screaming
                    into the blackening hills
compactly tucked & tubed like a small roll of
'love god'
            on the doorways of our rent due houses
            when we sit down

                            'o dont you know god is able

        when we walk down the beach

                        'he was moses
                            bush burning
                        & he digs you
                            real turning'

        & when we get high

who did we think we were who are we
now / y're tony, & frankie's frankie, &
i'm stuart &

                    'he's yr joy
                        & yr sorrow
                    he's yr whole
                        gone morrow
                    he's a hip
                        blasted starro

                        & he's able
                        to carry us
                        thru'

hey-ey! street gang of love lovers.  you & me
& frankie swimming elegantly down the promenade on
the mul
         ti
                colored jetting streams from the
     nozzles
of our dada noses
shouting & singing as though there were
no ears, how we have learned to use the roads
in & out of paintbucket poem veined
venice
           & each time
           dopes
           dreamers
once again convinced that
all angels & gasoline pump hearts
all crumpbacked organgrinding monkey dancing dwarfs
& bearded painters
& skinskulled painters
& tragic profile old movie style tango dancer poemprancers
will do what we know they can do, what they
never do, what we don't even know if they
want
to do

but we can overturn mop buckets in rage & watch
the lawyers & the lawyers' cocksuckers
the lawyers' righthand asswipers with the pink paper
the lawyers' lefthand asswipers with the white paper
the lawyers' apprentice asswipers with no paper issued them
yet

they hit the center of the makeshift stage
like tiny rubber toys, very small
they do the plastic man stretch as they reach
very high up over their heads into almost the
sun lite love lite life lite of dark of day or nite
reach to grasp & murder the tips of flowers
                    waiting
& there we are, / all three dressed like groucho

running up & down the sides of buildings for exercise
collecting these little creatures & jamming them into stuffy
key-holes dancing in front of the glassless mirrors
        of each others' eyes
                interchangeable
faces, souls, hands
this week tony can write with both hands for me & frankie
& frankie can paint with both hands for me & tony
& i will take care of diplomatic relations with the bourgeoisie,
                & the opposite sex


next show we do a skit where unbelieveably tall we rush
thru the front windows of the venice west cafe &
in perfect unison
doing a soft shoe ragtime
take deep breaths, squeeze the little bulbs
we hold unannounced in our hearts that push
the truth thru a narrow tube to where it connects
with our dopedeep eyes
& while they are looking into our bloodshot mouths
we will secretly
look love squirting all novelty shop into their empty hats


so, fellow dodomen, cliffclimbers
followers of the ancient undecipherable script
deliverers of whatever dangerous thing
it is that is thrust in anonymous brown commitment
under our arms on a rainy streetcorner where
we wait to be smashed by the lightning of the muse's laughter


we'll water pistol 'em
we'll seltzer bottle 'em
we'll love them if we can, & if we cant
we'll get high, & listen to the sounds & stories
inside the flat black plastic steamboat running pot smoking
                curling whirling round & round on
its phono porno philo graphic diamond dusted monk sound love

*Kowboy Pomes* (1973)

# ONE

given, even, the drive
is towards life, how
do they deal with it?

       the cock, the
cunt hidden. nobody sucks anybody
off.

whatever they do in their private mouths
dont interest me.

they ride into town
the heads of their horses high
their faces brown & windcracked.
i am not interested in their hands.
          everyone
has to come over the mountain, on
this side it's
no great thing.

       but what do they say of
fucking? of me? you? & all
the rest /
       churchbells
baseball
       crapgames
wooden buildings & mud
streets frighten them

i say it like an old sounding /
       who cant or wont chew
tobacco can hardly be expected to
suck a cunt, or to love
in any simple fashion

## TWO

cant see it. getting
in them wagons with everything
walking the cattle gut-gaunted
kids & women, too, i hear

       greed.  greed.
                hunger's
different.
            flowers that sing & stones that
bud forth shoots?
            hmph.  crawl
over a thousand
mountains
they wont find no
true word

i asked a stranger on a
salt caked horse
& he sd:  "never mind, y're
safe old
timer."


## THREE: ORPHEUS

i rode into town
my voice & my horse & my legs
one melted thing

looking
for it, you cd say.  dust in the nose
clogged runny eyes

i guess i smelled bad.   i
stank.  i smell bad now.   i
stink.

   to sing & be
home, two things dont
seem to come together

no one had to say
anything.  i just kept
moving, just keep moving

sometimes i think perhaps someone
will kill me.
    i look as fierce as
cracked tongue
permits.
    but it is the nature of
such places
not to be kind to
strange riders

   once, tho, they broke
my guitar.
now i have a
jews harp.


## FOUR: PEYOTE POEM


no wonder those bones
white dry in the
   limitless
hot space
   lie there.

they get to.

# FIVE: THE HEROES

1.

face to face.   is the gun
the poem?
is the sound the
poem, or the
echo?

face to
face.

   dancing in &
out of the four naked eyes
the whole thing jumbled, too fast for tally or
style

   the crumpled flesh, the birds that
hover for the invitation
of rot /
     something is
hidden, there, something
waits

2.

it is on consideration of time that
the past cannot blind
us, cannot bring the sweat
rigid on the body

as tho to say
there is now no sun
no dust
no street
no risk & need that dance in the shimmering air

no visions of distance & of
that face so close & deadly on our own


3.

i wd think to look
where the vultures look:   at the
meat.   the dead
flesh.   the broken face that
stalked & stared & took careful
watch, &
fell

at what even now
in these narrowed rooms
raises the smell of blood
to the nostrils


## SIX: PIONEER WIVES


women, women
you can crack that
whip, snap yr man
into place, slap the tobacco
from his mouth
buy sheep, build churches, sneer
at whores, wear
too many
clothes, whatever you
want / uplift, culture, you can even
give the place
                    *tone*

it's an economic law
about who's got what who wants

how badly
you all look very dignified in
old photos.
yr power shows in yr faces & yr men
are tired.

did you know you wd become
great harridans
with huge hats?
                        & look,
you never even
wiggled, just looked
martyred while he
did it
& now yr land is rotten & yr blood
is thin
yr faces are hard on the
faces of yr breed

                        only where there is still
space, yr smell
dont remind us all we
are strangling.

SEVEN: THE BUFFALO

1.

as tho it all
swung on
the belly, the
gut being core &
pulse.   the floor
of earth stinking
under its strange rug / rotting
flesh, stripped

naked.
man, who shivvers & is mostly
hairless, wraps in such
skin.
   yes, to be warm. not to say
it is good
to be warm, but
it is warm.
    but wore no
mask with horns, drew no
stark pictures, begged no permission
for murder. was not brother
to the flesh stink, the slam
sharp hoof
against the ground.

  after all, the
rails must be cleared, that's
money, the
crews must be
fed, that's
money.
   the heroes must be given
their strut & lie, their
validity.


2.


so much flesh: man & jackal
greedy feeding
gutswelling glutting
sniffing snorting stuffing
faces into it

blood irrigates, grass
grows thick, cows
munch, the
rest is known

rot fertilizes, wheat
grows.   steel
binds, the huge trains
bring touching
bring death
bring people
while he whose land it was
                (must still
        be)
is driven back by the stink
of decay.   that was his
manna, those herds, those
shaggéd wise heads.  meat his
unborn sons will cry for.
praying he has not committed
his gods to some evil thing
brooding over their own
deaths

his gods are warped
as his land is.   the great
beasts his brothers his food
all bloat & belch & fat
& mean flesh of
furious futility


3.

    what a gig that was. i dont know the wages, but each
morning into the unblooded sunlite white leather emblems
of virtue chewed soft by woman-tooth streaming straight
the wind. honor. carefully groomed, the beard, the mustache.

    to bring in food. fresh meat running blood down work
& laugh twisted faces. as tho the whole thing swings on
the belly. & honor.

4.

we are a naked race
humans our skins unlovely & worth
little.  makes good lampshades, is too thin
for practical purposes, so we steal
the skin & mount the great head & leave the flesh
behind. & hold our heads
high.  we have pride.

they sought water, & so
moved.  also the challenge of
horn to horn / those massive
heads clattered.  as tho all swung on
power.  & grass, who can
find it.  grass which
the great beast clump munched
like the one beast it was

indian hunters, after prayer
& dance hid within
sacred skins.  to see thru his eyes, crawl
to the core of his world
                              feed, sleep
nurse the young?  what of those
transformed
who never
returned, moving over the rich
land, eating
grass, begetting
grass eaters?

weight & balance.   the limits
long established.


5.

we put him on
money, stacked the money

71

into cities.   now
we have america
& the buffalo
live fenced they are
innoculated & counted
each year there is an official
hunt & buffalo roast
appears in select
butcher cases

proving the
marketplace has memory &
honor, tradition selling the beast's
haunch & eye, his name, giving him stance with
superman & firecrackers
the gut primary
the ear anesthetized eyes
right!  from metal
casts children
wd recognize him if his huge
head thrust thru electric doors
but he wd be sick as his
gods & brothers are, the buffalo
bird & buffalo flea
no longer with us or him.  new
parasites, new relationships.  no
space for him, anyway

even the coin he rides
so proud
dont buy much anymore.

*Alphabet* (1973)

 ALEPH

it is the man, himself
man
lord & master, the center
of his own
structured cosmology

it is
he is
the central point, the line
the direction taken
the road life walks thru his cells & stars

the power of the single
thrust, the pure
gesture of
self

its arithmetical value is 1

 BETH

a soft sound. a mouth
speaking. chanting. calling
the universe to account
for all pain / crippled growth / our world.

it is the entrance to
within himself, the interior
another
enclosed cosmos
protected
dark

who demands judgment?
man demands judgment
who is the victim?
man is the victim
who is the criminal?
man is the criminal
who is the singer?
man is the singer
who is the song?
who is the song?

its arithmetical value is 2

 GIMEL

within the cave, it is dark. safe
tunneled deep into the mountain. safe
in the womb

traveling the long passage, moving
like song thru the throat to ultimate shaping
we see
the fire, the lite, day, the brite openness
dancing. darkness fragments. all known
patterns dissolve into shifting brilliances

now voices are raised in fear
now questions echo from the walls of the enclosure
some insist only the flickering shadows have reality
they make their prayers a worship of measurement & reflection
some try to turn back, to the black
their chants celebrate blindness

it is a natural rhythm brings forth
all, all, spewed into the lite
to take form
to sing, cry, fear, dance, love, pray, move
to be
to be flesh
to be man
within the totality
of his functioning

its arithmetical value is 3

 DALETH

the warm source. where we
suckle & worship. nipples streaming
the power that nourishes.
all that lives must eat. perhaps
that which does not live
eats also. drinking from
other breasts. a symmetry of
hunger & transformation
from which flows
the fact of our abundant flesh
the world we touch & move thru
the whole physical universe

nuzzles here, at this firm
flesh assurance of joy & energy

its arithmetical value is 4

   HAI

the divine winds upon the waters
before there was lite & dark
before there was beast, man, angel
the winds
the breath
moved

the divine breath entered the clay
entered the stolen bone
to become
life. spirit & flesh
breathing, flowing, moving
the waters &
the generations

the rhythm of our lungs echoes the movements of the waves
all air is spirit in which the souls fly free
i breathe the souls of all the dead & all the living
i breathe the poisons which man feeds the winds
i breathe the power & the death
i take it in, let it out, take it in, i am revived, i am alive
the waters move & i am alive

its arithmetical number is 5

ו   VAV

that which sees: the eye
that which is seen: the lite

that which hears: the ear
that which is heard: the wind, speaking

that which hungers: the need
that which tastes: the need

all are balanced on this precise
point, where eye & lite combine
to banish darkness
ear interlocks with the songs of the air
hungers feed

from darkness
                    revelation
from silence
                    revelation
from hunger
                    revelation

its arithmetical number is 6

 ZAYEEN

the sound of a dropped
bomb, before it
hits, the long high shriek
piercing the air, opening the
air, before the earth
is erupted
is not language

the sound enormous exploding
fragmenting the stroke of the scream
definite, given, the point of
culmination
is not language

language demands
connections. delicate structures
must be firm
at the core

its arithmetical number is 7

 CHETH

from his perception of the fact of existence, man deduces
purpose, visualises direction. a consecrated journey. he
is driven by the hunger for its culmination. but he cannot
devote his energies solely to its achievement.

all is movement, direction is multiple. perspective alone determines who is going up & who is going down. at each point there are critical demands.

two hands must carry many tools. all concerns insist upon absolute care & the equilibrium of craft skills.

the gestures of reality demand attention. there is no lens thru which the patterns themselves are revealed. there is a flow from need to need. the sum of the actions is its own completion.

its arithmetical number is 8

   TETH


a secret enclosure
is the best refuge
walled, protected

demons of despair cannot enter
mirror-faced terrors cannot penetrate
frozen wind fingers cannot reach

it is safe. not thieves' hands
nor corruption's breath
can touch
what is kept here, watched over
guarded constantly
in its holiness

its arithmetical value is 9

**ר** YOD

with a thumb & four fingers anything can be held. the
hand. all power made visible in five fingers so structured.
history is the hand's fingers reaching, reaching for power.
history is the hand's finger pointing to the future. unknown,
unknowable. no tool held can carve its image. man as angel.
as debased monster. potential is infinite.

plato thot it designated
everything tender
& delicate

its arithmetical number is 10

 KAF

in the half-closed hand
is a fist
is a caress
is a tool
is a weapon
a hand raised in anger
searching
shaping & hanging on

a hand to put wedding rings on
a hand to touch
a hand with which to wave farewell to life as it passes

its arithmetical value is 20

ל  LAMED

the wing:
    i am an extension
    of the sky herself, who grasps
    the bird's hollow-boned flesh
    & flings it thru her vastness

the arm:
    i am from
    earth. i am her projection
    towards
    towards the sky
    towards god's face
    rooted, i reach

arm & wing:
    together we are interwoven
    to & from each other we move
    we join, separate, fly, grow
    rest as the bird
    on the outstretched branch
    sky feeding earth
    earth thrusting upward

its arithmetical value is 30

MEM

she is the mother
she is the lover
she is the mother
she is the companion
she is the mother
she is the friend
she stands unique

she is the mother
she is all giving
she is the lover
she is the source
she is the mother

she is the moon
she is the earth
she is the breasts
she is the blood
she is the sky
she is all flying
she is the trees
she is the food

she is both taken in & given out
she is both nourishment & death
she is all embracing & all forgiving
she is all tender & merciless
she knows & she does not forget

she is deceptive
she is seductive
she lies
she makes poems
she guards our lives from terror & gives ease
she destroys

she is She
she is She

its arithmetical number is 40

 NUN

here is
continuity. father to
son. this
is the son. the son
of man.
          living flesh
generation to generation
unending

it coils back upon itself
it perpetuates
it expands outward, encompassing
beginnings & endings

its arithmetical number is 50

 SAMECH


"sssssss" sd the glittering
slitherer. & the mother of us all
understood. & by her wisdom
gave us our knowing, our searching
gave us our whole turbulent awareness

all she took in return
was a weary burden, an endlessness
for which we are not strong enuf

a hiss that echoes thru our cosmos

its arithmetical number is 60

 AYEEN


sound, sound, noise, a chaos
of noise is trapped inside the head
by an intricate balance of
echoing tunnelways, thinnest
of membranes
resounding

        meaningless. a
jumble. the total
sound.

how then, does
it imply
everything crooked, low, perverted?

from confusion grows emptiness
from emptiness grows fear
from fear grows evil

its arithmetical number is 70

 PEI

the open mouth
thru which man makes himself
known. thru which
flows his inner world's voice
the songs of his spirit
the esoteric & the visible

its arithmetical value is 80

 TZADDI

impaled on the hook of god, man is
pulled towards his true becoming

this holy wound is carried
as the living staff of healing

he is pulled thru the waters of his own growth
a fish not to be eaten but to be transformed

protected in his seeking
knowing his ultimate

destination

its arithmetical value is 90

KOF

thru jungles of bones man stalks his family
tracing his history from the rocks
this letter implies the blackness of man's birthplace
the emptiness & terror from which his soul was formed
the ape, what we have left behind

but nothing is left behind, all is carried forward
on the threshold of angelhood
man will contain
his deepest beginnings

& none know
what will be lifted
to other levels

its arithmetical value is 100

 RESH

all questions resolve to one question: what is the real?
as we perceive it, within the head. making our sensing its
core.

from this point we move. the original centre, from which
radiates all direction. a standing alone.

its arithmetical number is 200

 SHEEN

contained within
the bow's tense string
is the impelling music to which
all souls, all stars
dance time's festive halls
gowned! perfumed! jewelled! the dazzling
patterns intricate & courtly
a sweet rhyme eternal

its arithmetical value is 300

TAV

rains fill the rivers which then fill the skies
man & the plants breathe mouth to mouth
who eats, is eaten, who feeds, is fed
giving & taking, a universal flow
this is the breath of life itself
flawless
unstained
forever
    resonant

its arithmetical value is 400

*8 april 1972 / 8 april 1973*
*larkspur, california*

## Only Just Above the Ground (1973)

> The true way is along a rope which is stretched not high in the air, but only just above the ground. It seems to be designed more for stumbling than for walking upon.
>
> —Kafka

# UNTITLED

hard to know
whether the place surrounds
or springs from my
own core

but has to touch, anyway
eyes closed or
running, dont
matter. the place, the
name, the hands
that hold
the thing made, they
come with

down
the nite, it
dont matter who
is crying. salt &
water, the
blinding lites
all that talking. these
do not vary

if birds fear
the gun, if the dead
cow fears the jackals
vultures, wild
dogs, we have no way to
know. only man is
human, has that inaccurate
tongue

yet my concern remains
the poem. i am pushed
to the edges, now they
leave me to my dyings

but the hands touch the
place. dirt sifts thru
the fingers. under the
arms it smells. strong

makes the place somehow a
woman, as most
things are. by which i
mean / to eat




## THE BARBARIAN FROM THE NORTH
*for Allen Ginsberg*


blind as roses
we sit in the evenings in rooms of our own choosing
rooms filled with intricacies of many delicately structured parts
which dazzle & fascinate, & alter appearances & statements

everything with its clear limits
everything marked & classified
all aspects known
all new structures viewed with distaste
everything of the utmost seriousness

what are we to say, then, of a man
who takes off his clothes in someone else's living room?
are we to applaud?
what is his nakedness to us?
what do we care about his poems?
do you realize that he is in the lite? how can i
be expected to read?

he makes too much noise!
he says dirty words!
he needs a bath!
he is certainly

drunk!

i hope he soon realizes that it is, after all
now
& we have many wonderful things to amuse us
when we want to see clowns
we go to the circus

*is he gone yet? can i come out*
*now?*


## "A BLOND FACE / A BLACK FACE / A NO FACE"
—James Ryan Morris

difficult to be
human.
no news that.

one known thing / pain
seems integral / unremitting

few still traversable
roads. dream
works erratic. the
poem, yes, another.

have to learn to expand
what doesnt want to.
risk.
limits, the limits
of pain.
i know no other
way. wearing
this face. you
wearing yrs.

pleases me because it's
actual / human to not
touch / to ease

a different mirror
is required. to see man
become an angel / his ultimate
destiny

it is a matter
of time. if only it were
not real.


## THE SUMMER: AN ELEGY
*for James Ryan Morris*


1.

the killers swarm the city
it is a summer madness
they look thru faces of mirror
they call my name

deep deep in the earth
the earth has eaten their bone
knives
their knives of bronze, stone axe honed axe
now their blades flash lite exactly as we have been taught
                                    to expect
secret pockets in their flesh
contain other weapons

i pretend it is my city
but they have full charge
of the graves
death is longer than life
this gives them their seniority & power

the blood in the summer
streets is
thick sticky as it dries in the sun
stinking like any animal matter
rotting for the children of flies

we are covered with it. with them. their blades
are steel. they flower
their own time & gesture. as nijinsky did impossible
*entrechats* as the flower's
ghost

graves now. flesh / eye / tongue
gone, only the bone remains


2.


mike magdalani, this yr
death poem. cdnt wait
for summer you killed in the spring, killed
mike magdalani
this yr death yr death
the poem of our
summer thru which the killers
move. under the full
moon or the half or any phase. even
a black sky or in the
rain which washes the blood into the soil where
grass bloats rust tinged gorging itself
on vein spill

row after row, flashing in the electric sun
a dance of thrust & slash

summer flares & thickens the rich flow

i pretend it is my city, as tho
love gives me the right to anything but
the act of loving
you did not wait
for them to seek you
out.  to take the
city with blades brite
& faces twisted

the summer
the hot summer
intensifies.  to touch scalds
flesh mike
mike this yr death

the knife / the knife / the knife in
the silver lite
it is polished with a knowledge of
the nature of edges.
at the end of the summer edges
draw in. there is no
protection there. they breed & swarm & infect.
it is too easy to be one of them.
how to kill.
if only it were not so difficult to distinguish
the faces.  why
is my mouth lowered
to the red river?
i see yr face mike bending
to the blood.
thirst will not be denied.

4.

mad mike the painter
became the first of the summer killers
murdered
mad mike the painter

he stumbled thru the streets
his body he hung like butchered meat in a window of his
                              stolen visions
he loved with fear
his killer head was shaved
they burned his warped & gorgeous brain with electricity
in the fury of his brush
he saw himself saint prophet
sent to paint the end of terror
wd have transformed all all
wanted man to suck his cock give him dope take as a simple
gift his eyes his eyes to see thru his eyes
to fly with his wings of dead birds

his eyes his eyes his hands
the visions that crippled them
he offered up as he
mad all the time whirling deranged desire stole
typewriters to
pay for june / as who hasnt / something
                              as bill burroughs sd:
'wdnt you?' you bet!

the killer goes direct / to the core / the root / where
                                        life is
my killer brother
strangled my own brother killer
as i might murder my brother
murder me
explode any flesh. even as my city
is exploded

graves / all graves
desolate my city my soul
desolate the fragments of my murdered brother
desolate the mirrors of blood
flowing the crude paths
between the burial mounds

the murderers
of children are among
us. disguised as clowns
& drunkards, they are often seen
carrying suitcases of unknown
content. they imperceivably
switch names, noses, worlds.
none have yet been apprehended. anonymous
they wear the human shape
with ease. as tho
it were their own.


## UNTITLED


1.


That which is
man. Called by that name.
With clumsy articulation
he pretends to sing. Not
hearing its aged laughter, he
cultivates the earth. He has gods.
They wear his face.

Structures man builds, intricate
graphs he draws, speak to him
in his own words / that he is a
pinnacle, a completion.

The gods made of mirrors cannot
hide the clenched fist. Bloody,
it is his OWN arm.


2.


Clever at changing his shattered masks
he hides the process from himself. Purified
man is his only
vision as he crushes ants.
His proud walk prevents his
seeing himself a collection
of separate animals. Gross in his own
image, he is their functioning.
He sees a moving thru
time / himself its ultimate
Something will be pleased
when his image collapses. That
the struggled climb
was no waste.
Turn over for Absolute Revelation. The Mysteries
are known.

As time
is, as history is.


3.


Only Jews have concern with
this. & those whose function
is to be their murderers.

As time
is counted by the counters
of time.
The river within the flesh, what
hides there? A Jew knows
he is a Jew. A fact also known

to his destroyer? Known
in the unknown ocean, the encompassing
river? The Nourisher, the Killer?
The blood?


## UNTITLED


machine gun the belly of a crowd. winter
protects, the murderers sleep. even it is cold.

some things last, some dont seem to. what hurts is
true. can be touched. touches.

in cities bells ring. history is blind as it touches
the mouth.
even at best the race don't seem solid.
here. i have little faith in it.

## How It Is, Doing What I Do (1976)

*first please for a word: we were going to do this book stuart & me, it was planned. time past things happened. i took a year w/stuart's journals finding how it is a man can paste his life together. its been gd for me: its being lucky for the chance. the riddle of the one who lasts & the duty of remembering. its not so much the man u love but what he sd & showed u. it is not unique. every one shld have a stuart in their lives. what a zest & energy to get it done. this is how he did it: he believed.*

*these poems are all the ones that he had chosen. 'voices heard in venice'\* was written around 1957 when he was being pulled out of his jimmy yancey bag & listening to monk & mingus. the rest of the poems are all from 64 & 65. 'how it is doing what i do' i find thru out those journal years many working pages until he got it down the way he wants. the how it is poems are most important tellin how it was doin what he did. this is what i like abt a message. u learn & u dont even know it. all the rest is pages from his journals. every nook was started w/an invocation. the one i chose is an example: the lady is important to the book. the books are covered w/quotes as were the walls in all the houses that he lived in. history & responsibility: u will tell the others what u know. this then is partly how i say my debt. the rest is how i live it.*

*t. scibella*

---

\* Here incorporated in *The Venice Poems* as printed below, p. 255.

*UNTITLED*

o muse, i beg you, fill
this book as my life is filled
may no words be here until
you yr fury have stilled


HOW IT IS, DOING WHAT I DO

I

undetected i am
sly i with certain
skills look at humans i move
next to & against

when i walk i look downward
left right left right fast foot dance
movement pavement beneath
with caution & knowledge
i walk a tunnel
thru the world

distances between seem to be growing greater
that cd be aging
that cd be my own fragmented self
that cd be a reaching for
bird wing stroke in vast sky

it is difficult to give them Her
joy, their joy. in their subtle
disguises. their masks imply other masks
& perhaps weapons

the intent remains / She gives words
to the voice, for
them / moving moving
                                    it
is theirs. what is built. to make
a touching
a love
            one
gives, one
receives. She
is praised. i
am filled.

i am constantly trying to invent devices
tools ruthless & chaos
games made of warped mirrors, rigged
to pass
the gift. its weight. its needs.


                    II

opening day is limitless
& grey. all nite
those around me exchanged
gestures with me / a dance
that imitates love

a morning of machines
a morning of speed
a morning of strange lands

with no sun
no warmth
my prayers are for gulls
& to see the ocean, feel its
life. i need. my hunger screams.

but they are here, locked
in steel. they move in terror.

i cannot see them.
do they have faces?
the world is blank & dull. i pray
for gulls & water, prayers
purely selfish.
here where i shd speak
i am cowed & muted.

      how it shd be:   see
      what is real
      invent it
      transform it
      then one voice one pulse
      Her ecstasy

      but this
real, these
machine man hand
owned hand owned tool hard steel
fast poisoned air
noise grey day thru which we hurtle
all real
brings fear
it is no longer possible to pray
to think of birds.
exposed. all protection a memory.
i have no mask. my knowledge
applies to something
totally different
i try to forget what i carry
i cannot reach them
machines cannot be changed into angels
grey days give no heat
the sun's praises remain unchanted
all mirrors i see show no face
i am faceless steel
a thing of this world

# III

1.

the natural object
says old ez
is the best
symbol, the
best

    poems are made
of words, the word is not
the object, the thing
to make of words real
faces speaking actual
human worlds / something
a poem does. Her
thing. one of
Her things

poetry does not alter the path
of any movement, auden says
but in the same poem he prays it
will heal his grim visions
warm his gaunt & naked
flesh

words are crude, words
are lies, but She
is subtle, She is devious.
She has Her own desires & demands
She needs the word
structure. what it can do.
with it She makes all gesture an act of dance
in which the dancers can be moved
together, moved
to touching

all things real

not a prophetic vision
a matter of history
the poem one tool She uses. with its
poets. & its words


2.


the object
the best
She likes
poems made
of what is. is real.
at the core of what i do
is the Muse. She
the source / Hers the flow / my human
hands attempt to shape
it, to learn
to shape it
to Her purpose
as i am owned & used &
transformed by the very craft
i learn to use to see Her
rage appeased. to make
a precise
tool. the accuracy
of Her needs


3.


one nite i saw Her in the sky
arms widespread to me
the peyote was alive in me
i cd see the full moon & the cloud
formations / the real things She built
Her image of

               & once She was in fire
burning in private ritual

poems written to be burned for her
an act of homage invented by frank rios

specific
two times
chronological
i have
undeniable
seen Her

i record only fact
i offer things of weight & substance in evidence
my testimony has the authority of my total craft experience
i receive, as a gift
i form words to transmit
i do not originate
i do not choose


4.

i am greedy & lucky
to attract Her attention
i have survived disasters at the edges
i pray sing chant gibber moan beg
i knock on wood three times
i worship the moon, the sea, human
woman / Her presence
as female

that She gift me with poems
each time a new thing
out of my exalted hands

# IV

1.

the Lady tells me
once again
to speak of love
again again

She knows the death-lust such speech beckons to me
it floods ungulfs drowns with
my bitterest flow / how
i kill myself
to believe
while building
that i know
a shape with sure hands searching
to glut with pleasure
on another's belief
that my poems visions gestures revelations say
what is the real
this power is death to me

i almost died of power

then 'he' is
released / the me
who finds such
pleasures

i am obliterated if his is
he trys to become each time more secretly
the face in my mirror


2.

i was very young
i knew nothing
contemporaries, other 6, 7, 8 year olds

brought their pain to fat boy jew boy me
i knew i knew only
nothing. perhaps
it became known that later in life
i wd grow a mustache

they came to me
i only saw
their needs, demands, their hungry act
of coming
          to me! why did they
come to me?
i found no reason for it
they were not interested in the
question. to me they came
i thot i was supposed to know
i knew nothing
they gave me their pain
to know, to ease, to help
carry it. their actions sd
i did know. they taught me
to believe it

power. i almost died of power

those who came to me with love
who love me
have often become addicted to such destruction

power / my tool for many dyings


3.

now i know i do not know
i am not healer
i am not sewer
knowing Her i know me
human. was near death
with power when She gave me

this knowing this
tool
weapon
patterns
structures
transformation

     a not quite doing it

     the simple gesture, its grace made
     rhythm


4.


all reality alters not only that
a poet touches even
the body
totally different

i am not clever. power
may yet destroy me. i show
who i am
what i speak i know true
in my own flesh true
clumsy i somehow see


5.


i go seldom into the streets. i am unprotected there.
i stay in my room. the walls surrounding
written with words from
obscure tribal lore
secrets of witchmen
charms
totems
formulae of invocation

a shelter. a safety.

Her concerns differ. love
must be spoken.
for Her that is my function.

i almost died of power
i almost died of words
almost died of structures
& more, more, any risk
that She use me
to mould the
molten lethal metal
in my hands


V

1.

i love a woman who is in pain
but i cannot take it into myself
into my love for her
cleanse her of it. no. there seems
a limitless supply of pain
enuf for everyone


so alone
love does not rupture the isolate barriers
within which we are


2.

i remember being in a garden
thick green & heavy twisted jungle of love
air heavy with smells of color & singing
others were there, everyone, we plunged ahead,
                            we trusted all paths
that there be no quicksand
that there be no snakes, spiders, maggots, vermin

that there be none who eat flesh among the inhabitants

we hurled ourselves thru thorn clumps
rested in dark caves
ate whatever the mouth cd find
knowing the destination, knowing its value
having seen it, having been there

on one of the very real worlds thru which i have
                              travelled i discovered blackness
i looked around me & cd see no one
in that single skin i saw no faces, no touching
i remembered man's shape, i remembered the visions
but in that dark i had
only words. in an unmapped garden. unknown jungle.


3.

the Lady needs real things
to make poems
as Her collector i have
developed an eye of practiced suspicion, wary
of all things seeming to be. with this eye
i watch my human pretty as she sleeps
this morning she sleeps clothed
but often she is white
naked flesh woman flesh in the morning
real flesh real ecstasy bodies
flesh loved flesh
touched flesh kissed bitten petted
my body
her body


4.

we have this love in a room we hope is safe
at the edge of a city enormous with enemies
i think we are illegal under the old statutes

we may decorate the walls, but expect their collapse
at no specific time, any time, constantly


5.


growth is change
everything changes
& betrays. murder
is not enuf
like love / both
human, both present
in the hands we use to caress & to pray


# THE JUGGLER


when presumed by his parents to be masturbating,
he practised in the secret closets & bathrooms of his
childhood. he threw objects into the air, seeking patterns
from the random twitch of impulse. every existing physical
thing has its own weight, he believed. to discover this
weight, its patterns, in the solitude of his deceptions he
flung things into the air, each movement unknown, a
release, a giving over.

what a task he undertook with his sweaty armpits!
to displace desire! to re-invent mirrors! to invent new
lusts! prodigious!

now, there he is. dazzler, enchanter. evoker of order.
he presents himself to us. it is a hero's gesture. he receives
admiration, wonder, hunger, worship, mockery, denial—also,
love—love? yes! even love he receives as his just tribute. so
much so that such offerings are collected in weaves of
straw during intermission, by an underling. he is not

troubled with it. he has earned the dignity of his gestures
of simulated rigidity.

on the stage platform, elevated, separated, isolated
with the purity of the light, he is strong, a pattern of
generation & return, deathless in its perpetual freshness.

but who muffled his hurt whimpers when his flesh
was smashed clumsy by falling things? who gave him
verification when his mirror reflected only decay, despair,
delirium, when form was indistinct, perhaps only a lie
of disintegration? when he knew there was no balance,
when his own mouth cursed him, when his eyes became
clogged with malignant fungus, then he was alone in
the desperate retreats of the shadowed alleys.

he panted, gasped, wheezed for oxygen. his head
he leaned against the hot abrasive brick. gulped at the air.
there was not enuf oxygen in the air. the light crackled
on his skin like bursting hot grease. its hard glare, its
erratic shifts of emphasis, confused his vision. he waited
for the inevitable enemy to emerge from the light, leap,
swift strike, punish.

no one waited with him. he waited alone. he had
no choice.

that was the place where he was made naked,
stripped of skin, skein of deceptions—all we weary carry
& defend ripped from flesh, from bone, from wound,
which recoiled, drew back, white & lustreless in the so
bright sun. the cowering flesh revealed & betrayed.

he was there, & survived to become his own being.
surged onward, to his craft, his being accepted by others.
yet he is isolated, removed from us, hemmed by the
boundary of the lights.

has he supervised this arrangement, so as to make
more likely the continued banishment of the beast

vindictive met & defeated once in the shadows? it wd
be an understandable precaution.

but this is the juggler, whose every gesture of
impossible symmetry weaves a dance of balance, a denial
of chaos. he has faced the anger of the Earth Herself,
who wishes only to embrace all things, to draw in towards
Her the solidity of all physical presence. he has faced
what he has faced. he knows the extent to which he is
protected.

i believe he is set away from us in order to minimize
the risk of anyone's—myself, perhaps—inadvertently finding
himself in total & direct confrontation with the dance of
order & balance. for each fragment of thrust & fall, touch
& withdraw, color & song, so fits into its proper place as
to become one shimmering, flawless thing—balance containing
all possibilities—a mirror, a clarification. what one looks at
is really there, & one sees.

but no surface, no matter how polished & crafted,
has been known to reflect images of the dead, who move
always among us, who move even within the blood boiling
in the veins. wearing, as murderers, any face as mask.

we look at him, & see only his bright dream. no
reflections. the management & various authorities do not
want us to know we have no reflections in his pure mirrors.
they disguise the fact with music, flashing colors, shifting
scenes & locations. in this way we see only him, not missing
the reflection of our images, the absence of which we are
unaware. we are moved, & offer him all possible gluts to
any conceivable hunger.

but when he looks at us, he no matter how masked
& bewildered his stance, must see that which the mirror
refuses to reflect.

if he had known, in his anguish, what awarenesses
precisely he was earning, i wonder what visions of

perfection wd have been of sufficient power to make
him seize the beast while he prayed for death &
deliverance.

which prayers the Lady in Her own way has
granted you, o prancer of miracles, o twirler of jumbles,
trapped & embraced by the patterns of flood, of
invention of chaos.


## THE SONG OF THE SECRET POLICE

our times are fast
they're crowded
we're crushed
we're lost

mirrors are broken
i.d. cards torn
faces are stolen
disguises are worn

no order! all chaos!
all turmoil! no peace!
but we can rely on the secret police!

man's own face repels him
he doesn't know his name
but he knows that someone
is scoring the game

in the black of the nite
in the uniform terror
wrong is judged! right is right!
this hell is no error

there's a plan
    we cant see it

even man
    cannot flee it

no order! all chaos!
all turmoil! no peace!
but we can rely on the secret police!

man destroys himself with power
he is desperate, confused
minute by minute, hour by hour
he sees his offerings refused

each failure is another crime he carrys
of millions on millions on millions of crimes
he lies to himself in his storys
but these *are* criminal times

no order! all chaos!
all turmoil! no peace!
but we can rely on the secret police!

## UNTITLED

man, with all his knowledge, does not know
how to make living less forlorn.
is it really better, as some have sd
never to have been born?

at birth, for each, all seems possible
from there, without interruption
life cd flow towards fulfillment
instead of towards destruction

man's flesh, his soul, his dreams & visions
race to their ultimate, total, rot
while he directs his energies
towards making what is, & is not

to most, life seems an enemy
exploding, crumbling, attacking, descending
racial survival is ruthless, indifferent, faceless
there is no touch, no interchange, no blending

all die. this fact startles no one.
what does it matter?
even so, does it not seem
a man's life cd be made better?

## UNTITLED

dancing is the body's secret
flower burst sudden! open! impossible
bloom from flesh enclosed
the body embraces itself, marking
its own severe limits
violated! shattered! flowered into
it is a celebration
it celebrates itself
the dance, the flesh
the colors of the flower, how it smells
the movements of the warm flesh blood pulse
throb of dark
juices flowing
gestures ancient & sacred in animal hunger

dancing the body denies itself
nothing. it knows only
joy! joy! the ecstasy of flesh
locked in its own mystery

it sings to itself
songs only flesh can touch
singing its own blindness

the body dances / dancing, the
body becomes the
flesh flowering. flowering
in dance the body is
the body's
is the body's secret
is the body's secret flower

## A SUGGESTION TO MY FELLOW CITIZENS

imagine revolutions have occurred! yes! why not?
& revelations! more! love! more! communal joy!
forget the rules, the rulers, the restrictions
which limit every action, every flight
of grace & wing. create
instantly yr ideal
city! its market places stocked
with fulfilled desires wrapped in images
unknown, but known to be
lovely as yr selves. extend yr arms & dreams
& see how interlaced a web
is structured by yr separate human needs.

## *UNTITLED*

the brass monkey earns his balls
it takes terrible cold to
freeze them off

in alchemy, brass is the holy
metal of potency
of power
another fact:  it is a cold world
cold cold cold may be cold enuf
to scare that monkey as he
watches the cold bloom in eyes
who do not look at
his threatened balls, nor
at the cunt itself, nor
the asshole juices flowing hot meat
devourers

cold enuf?

even our hands exchanging gifts
are reflected in the mirror
i cannot deny the mirror
it contains the face
it is a cold gleamed edged thing
a doorway never warm enuf to
lean, & nod in

warm enuf?
warm enuf for you?


## UNTITLED


human blood is its own
cartography. man knows
the distances, alone
& huge within the flow
islands of purity
great caves of death embraced
by flesh, the map of history
on which all pain is traced.

the flesh is muscle-clamped to bone
bone on bone on bone, to structure
a bone cartoon, which strives to make
a balanced tension, prone to rupture
on feet unlikely for their function
their stolen shape twisted, the horse
whose hooves they were, extinct. he found
them too clumsy to pace the course.

"my meat eats me" says roethke. i eat it.
eventually everything is food.
all life is dying, death is life completed.
in the same flesh, living is death renewed.
a flow of generation & return
more deathless than man's lust
to be divine. yet rage & terror burn
man's blood bubbling the dust.
flesh is not taught to trust
enormous rhythms. nothing it can learn
from what it holds within itself denies
the foredoom of its own decay. flesh dies.

## THE MAN OF MANY METALS
### for Don Martin

deep in the earth, at a meeting point of many veins
of ore & rivers of stone, the man of many metals dug &
hollowed his home.

he drew his materials from the earth in which
he burrowed, &, using his vast knowledge of the arts of
transmutation & shape, he made a room of brass & iron
& jade & ebon stone & ruby steel, multi-metal-mirrored
for his homage.

the actual building of his cave demanded many
years of work & study, & upon its completion he found
himself in possession of such skills & wonders as demanded
to be used by the simple fact of his possession of them.

with humble ecstasy of dedication he began what
he hoped wd be a life-long project of total self-realisation
by making for himself, out of various combinations of
metals known only to his magic, a new hand, with which,
with much delicacy & care, he replaced the hand that had
been for all his life his left hand.

this truly spectacular accomplishment he received
as a gift. shaken with awe, he watched as the hand itself
turned off all the lites in his sanctuary.

it was the complete darkness of under earth. he
struck thumb against finger, creating a single brite orange
white flash spark of lite which he captured in the shifts
& glints of jewel cut shimmered surface of his new hand.
he bounced it off the mirror-brite walls, off his eye, then
caught it flashing again in his hand. the absolute blackness.
the single spark, kept brite & warm in his metal embrace.

in this way he began to know the true nature of
his flesh.

ABT MIRRORS

mirrors have no hidden secrets
mirrors overwhelm with their accurate semblances
mirrors wear the mask of absolute verification
mirrors are surface & image, they testify
                              only to the surfaced image
only a mirror can check out a mirror

mirrors are known to be soft entrances to death
                              & gloved hands
mirrors are known to be soft
mirrors are not insistent, the images are
                              emptied of depth & validity
the mirror does not set the mirror in any place,
                              any relationship
mirrors do not deny their hunger to eat the image
the mirror does not barter, it wants all

mirrors reflect all equally
they are well trained to mirror mirror images

a mirror can be killed, but not mirrors, not mirroring
mirrors demand i accept their image, for there it is
in mirrors what is looked at is seen, it is there
mirrors whirl & flash sunlite
mirrors distort by their accurate denials
mirrors are black, black mystery, alluring, tempting
in mirrors all is shown to be lies
the mirror is strong, where words are, it is silent

in mirrors i see a face not my face! faces!
                              changing! not so! lies!
mirrors are unreliable
                              shifting! dazzling!
                    flashing! glittering! twirling!
mirrors will not be doors
mirrors will not show me my face
i do not know my face
only the mirror knows, it imitates my face,
                              my real face
mirrors divert attention from the real by
                              being mirrorgleaming
mirrors show no illusions. they show nothing
                              of blindness
they will not show me my face

i search the mirrors for something i've had
          in my pocket a long time

# THE GULLS, AGAIN

        the simple
impress. it might be
bird, wing, flight, glut
on the sand the
tide emptied of fish, of food

structures, built things as they
the helicopter noise shattering their ritual rest
rise rise as a group
circle in air with their wings
moving almost not
moving around to settle almost
as before

with their harsh song complete
homage / strut of self
power / recognition. this ritual
when the sun comes thru the clouds
is repeated with joy with
i can see they are
laughing

*Visions For the Tribe* (1976)

there are many people who know Stuart—
some as poet, some as a man; but few as both.
i have been one of the privileged few
to know both, the poet & the man.

i saw great chunks of visions   pouring forth
out of the chaos he made order from.  the poems
pounding out rhythms, riding the backs of gulls
into the lite of vision; always paying homage
to the lady, mother of the poem, believing
himself a tool to be used as she saw fit.

he followed her sounds along the edges
of tomorrow's dance . . . he always said
"be careful poets! it's hers, she can take it back."

his total dedication to his craft touched
within himself  the core of the poet as man
transformed . . . the human natural flow, growth.

    "i have been touched by her,
    she has spoken thru me, appeared,
    gave me the poem, a most sacred
    trust, to record"

I know down deep in the belly of my heart
if i had not known stuart, walked with him,
had not loved him, & him me, i would not be
a poet  entrusted to receive her poems.

like a knight riding thru the world of dragons
stuart penned his visions, found within his own
core the truth, ripped it out thru flesh & soft
bone the poem like a child's cry, coming to life.

stuart is dead now by the dragon's cancer,
but we know that he lives on in our hearts
& surely in these poems.

                 frank t. rios

# INVOCATION

lady, i implore you
take my hand
& we will go together
lady
over the land

     i have seen yr face
shining full over the black
mountains, a holy eye in the air
a brite call
a shout of joy
     i give you homage, lady
freely, wholly
    let us walk

lady, the trees stand
clustered in council
like gods / tall
strong. in the distance rain feathers like
black chalk
down the bluebellied sky
over the land

remember my eye, lady, what can i see?
my eye is yr eye
    holy eye
       brite love scream
in the sky

lady, humbly, i beg you
take my hand
guide my eye, lady
over the land
lift my vision
my cloud drunk blood

i want to ride down the feathers of love, lady
to where the rain strikes the fat earth
& mixes
& is mud


## ON RETURNING TO VENICE


time is confused on the streets of my city
returning, it is now & always as i walk
thru footsteps of memory

fog limits vision, & my eyes turn
inward, where birds fly the feet
over paths of intricate memories

ghosts over my shoulder do not push or press
rather, their eyelessness peers to pierce
the veiled images of the future, or
the flowers ballooning from the clouds of mist


2.

all is not voice
or vision. real walls
separate the rooms
within which movements
are limited by
space. & the bodies
within it

what endless histories
walk each separate flesh
each mind touching
its own
chronology

which goes beyond, encompasses
boundaries & isolations
within rigidity
the flow of continuity


3.

o ghosts
o my past
the face i wear

o my city
my flesh
the space given

yr voices in my ears
yr tears in my eyes
hands touching
songs ringing
from room to room
in the houses of my mind

## QUEEN OF HEARTS

*for, & after a painting by, Ben Talbert*


The queen totally
immersed of hearts red white blue the queen
of hearts
& cunts

        her own so open, so
        there, exactly where
        it is as not to be
        deep nest in her playing card thighs

        meticulously more a cunt
        than humans know tho not
        spelled out for children
        line by line
                    it is structured
        of dark incoherence its
        red white blue world the mouth
        suck hungry wet for its
        undeniable presence

america! america! exact
bands of color divide the eye the stars
so placed to name known the banner it is
america!          seen
by this eye made by this
this particular
america! america!
hand.     red her nipples, her face & attitude
all have known, or
touched / bar, backseat
nuptial bed

2.

romans were taught to choose any
dying to retain the flags
of their immediate reality.  all flag red is
rooted in their blood.  enclosing here
a history of revelation, future, being.  games
of cards  /  they are
war, the
card, the game,  shaping
man,  compressing
his chronology

it is need she speaks
to, excites.        to
fuck, to know
the future, to be
one with what the banner
intends as meaning, such
promise to enrich my
world social power money danger hatred
love world she pretends for us to be
part of.      integral.

                    love is
blinded red white blue nation people
the flag.              love  /  to be what
is shared.   red
white blue fortune or
game queen embraced.      america!


3.

the painted red is red
but different
the not white pearls a live grey
the blue its own
life its leap to the
eye its vitality

                              no such power
symbol her mysterious accurate cunt
to be found only
here her slut face in america
a born liar held safe
the painting the physical
limit & protection


her cunty queen-ness hard pounding tits
supposed to signify
passion  /  the heart.   i feel
no desire but recognize the
magic  /  it comes from
tarot the magic
painted, the power in
the taut canvas thing.   locked
there anyone might be
safe might not be safe



4.


america a debris
of emptiness passed thru two strong hands
squeezed shaped placed each
in its right
relation to all
america
cunt
queen
america
of hearts
red white blue
this painting

# LETTER FROM PRISON

they told me i am not
who i am
& i wondered, because
there are so many of them
with loud voices &
documentary evidence & clubs & statistics

maybe that was why
          (being
     the wrong me)
i hurt so much.
it was confusing

i found out
(no need for details
 of this craft
                    i really am
who i am
     (so many years
watching the shaping & growth
getting
     as much as i cd, cd learn to
     my hands into it
can see they are
who & what they appear to be
not
     (no surprise this
          what they say

now there is this
clarity / that i know
where this who i am is
          here
in this thickness, suffocation
each breath, each thot, each
seeing like rocks on my

back, bones in
my pack

but even
everything falling
in place
(on me, maybe, but
where each thing fits
doesnt seem
to make a real
balance

will it all
(is this hope
foolish?
some day be as structured
& whole as any chronicle
or nitemare?


POEM/LETTER
*to James Ryan Morris*


I am Thinking abt Kenneth Patchen
I am writing Too many poems to the dead
I am Thinking of Kenneth Patchen
I am Thinking of my dead wife Jana
I am thinking of Billy Batman
of Roethke, of Bessie Smith, of
William Carlos Williams
of Paul Carleton, of my Grandmother

She was so Tired

"I Think God has forgotten me." she sd

lists of the Names are not appropriate memorials

I sing the loss, praising the Living Continuity,

                                                    but it

weighs heavy to my hand
Thinking of the absent
loved ones


## ODE TO INCONGRUITY


with only two feet
we manage to walk
up this street
down that one
turn / a country road? the signs
are in a different
language (isnt
everything?)

with only two eyes
we manage to see
simultaneous projections
multi-shifting revels
gauze, canvas, brite lites
accurate representations
birds
perhaps, even
reality

with only two hands
we manage to touch
skin is soft, when touched
flesh yields
even the
immaculate bone becomes
flexible
gentle

with only one mouth
we invent confusion
we sing speak form
words words
shaped sounds inadequate
obsessive
endlessly flowering


2.

learned men
assure us
(with full footnotes)
that all
is very meaningful & complex
is overwhelming & structured
is devised & categorised
can be
understood
integrated
substantially defined
verified
by cross-referenced
indexes

it is official
two feet / one street
two eyes / one image
two hands / formal gestures
one mouth / prescribed responses

all documented
with refutable
graphs

3.

if we walk down
the world reading
obscure maps & trailing
endless fluttering lists
of rules & directions
we will fall into the crevices between realities
eyes fixed on the known
we will stumble into
a wall
a flame
a distant cosmos

surprise! joy! revelation!
survival demands
laughter
quickness
agility
juggler's hands
& devious dreams


THE CLOWN


1.


into a world waiting hungrily
he falls
            in a world reversed
he stands on his head & asks
        "who is upside down, you
         or me? whose nose
         is out of shape?"

children do not laugh at clowns
a clown laughs
& a child opens all his eyes

two for the world to look into
one to see the clown with
& one, most secret eye
with which to peer inside the world
where the head walks along the floor


2.

on a wire stretched across
the eye of a child, a figure teeters

suddenly!
it!
falls!

it bounces upward!
it falls again!

the wire snaps
the trumpets melt in noise
it was a clown
only a clown!

the clown moves in & out of death
& the children shiver & turn pale
their wires hold
their frightened mouths emit
no sound

two eyes close
two see the clown sway on
until the death of childhood

3.

the world of a circus
is ruled by clowns

the bloody white
the bloodless red
the fat dead nose
these are
portions of a map in
the child's geography

as he falls on his face
                screaming
            "who is upside down, onlooker?
            whose pants dont fit?"
                                he dances away
    from life, &
                the children, they
                    (some follow
                know



CRAFT NOTES:  FOR H.E.


it is the same energy
which makes yr hand tremble
which makes yr nipples harden
which charges the poem itself
the poem itself a thing of flesh
as you are. a structured
organism, warm, filled
with growth & pain
needing & satisfying its needs
finding its own
unknown rhythms

the poem takes all into itself
as a living being, as you
to find & be nourished
to illuminate & to understand
to have place, thrust, meaning
to be alive
the flesh the poem the human
ecstasy


## UNTITLED


totally tender, you
open & flowing, nourishing
me. in my need
my need animal & real, trying
to breathe. to breathe freely.

even tho we (you, also) are
crippled by our being
human. that is its
strength, its joy, its
extravagant flowers


## UNTITLED


we are forced to wage war
against time

yr head a soft black mountain flower
growing
wild against the pillow

is illuminated midst
the rubbish of love

the thing almost slips away
into the hands of the clock
but
we can move very slowly
filling you full


THREE PRAYERS


1.

o do not let our children
as you let us, grow
without the help of hatred

do not let the violence of their souls
destroy their souls
let them sing it out

against us?
            what else?


2.

grant that the walls may fall
catching within their ruin
all the ones who've lived in sanctuary
& from their vantage point have
grabbed us
pumped into
our blood
a hideous drug of their own invention,
                        & forced us to beg them

to accept us
while we despised
them &
ourselves

   grant that the walls may get them
as they now have us


3.


a personal prayer / let me have the strength
to make the scene
& still not harshly warp
my true sound

let me gain power over that power
that tries to kill me

loosen the root of death within my head
& let me get my hands on it, & pull, & pull


NOTES ON BODIES


1.


making a poem of
bodies / one next to
another, piled high, dead
poems of war
poet generals in love with
death & the abstractions of national
pride

2.

sing! sing! the body's
liberation into joy
acceptance of needs & flesh
human & holy

let us touch / touch our selves
each other's
selves
all, all, everything included
death & pain, oppression & grief
in our physical
transcendence


3.

the body's history
is all history
the body's reality
is all reality

flesh, our limit
our infinite
cosmology



*UNTITLED*


over my prayer shattered head
the morning sky unfolds its secret lite
of delicate cloud pink blood from the muse's soft veins
                                 & birds
brushed rapidly crying onto the air

the moon our lady, seen thru softest colorkisses
loses her sharpness of shape, dissolves, expands to
          fill the last of nite blood in the sky with naked
                                        awe

in the silence of the unawakened city
not yet conscious of its drained & murdered canals
not yet flooded by the lowering of the gates of money
not yet
bought & sold & raped & cheated its this day's thousand
                                        times
moves softly, a huge cat stretching perfect feline grace of
                                        body
the pigeons purring the warmth of its deepest throat

my feet greet the oceanfront walk with
the breathheld notquite real
impact of the returned lovers breasts

& at my side i feel the heavy physical presence
of the walking she walks with me thru my eyes


UNTITLED


the beach is cluttered with garbage & debris.
time dies. the sun is setting. it is evening.
the ocean is enchanted, the hushed waves sing
a song of peace, of rest, of serenity.
the gulls move without effort, joyously
thru the still air. Cool breezes bring
foretaste of night. the earth's breathing
pulses the sand with the rhythm of the sea.

gentle the sound, gentle the breeze, gentle the wash of the surf
gentle the voice of the child, the air filled with her chatter.
gentle the sand that makes my body a part of the earth
gentle the sun, its setting, its rich redness on the water.

each day brings this gift, the peaceful time /
but where are the dancers? where are the worshippers?
                    where is the sacred rhyme?


## UNTITLED


what to me is so
good
is how you are
so brite with being that
young warm thing.
alive, it says
alive alive


## MOON SONG


the moon is round & fat
with silver lace
across its face
& magic in its hat.

the moon is white & brite
she has all art
within her heart
& dances in the nite.

the moon is many things
the poet knows
that she bestows
the very songs he sings.

the child sees a jewel
but then, one day
it goes away.
ah! how moonly cruel.

another evening sky
& it appears
a slice of tears
with laughter in its eye.


## ODE TO SADNESS

it is not
loss. what has
been, is. the
future is only
hoped for. a door
closes, there is
darkness. in
the dark, pain
silently
silently
enters my head
squeezes my eyes
from within
changing images
on paintings
still locked
in hands
sounds of poems
unwritten

fall back
to
silence
silence


*UNTITLED*


i have ten fingers that twitch
spasm a peculiar dance
out of
     rhythm, out of
           (not quite
focus

that are not keystone kops chasing fat blond girls all
     smiling the same mouth all sucking the same
cock
are not the master destroyers / fields
     putting the obviously unfunctional steering wheel
     into his passenger's hands
     zooming miraculous speeds on a mountain road

          chico
     annhilating a piano, fragmenting it, splinter shred
          ripped seams

          harpo
     plucking the sounding board, his eyes dreaming in
     to some unforeseen somewhere

          the laws
     of space & time denied as uncounted millions
     cram into groucho's famous stateroom

all the masters of malediction have their structures
& patterns

but my muse starved fingers twitch erratic
unrhythmic as
they stroke a soft breast
grip pen or brush
or jerk miserably loose & ashamed in my pockets, at my sides
or whenever i reach for, or
touch


## FOR A FRIEND'S MARRIAGE


the flesh sees
the flesh seeks
hungry, the flesh feeds on
the flesh

the shambled structure of bone
& meat, the body
containing more than its own
demands, reaches, remembers
even in isolation
locked into itself
enclosing itself
screaming within its own impassable
boundaries, remembers
old words, old knowledge
in the blood, maybe, in the prayers of vision
that two such distant monsters, human
can be
can become
"one flesh"

touching hungry the flesh
feeds on the
flesh song, body singing, mind & vision
dancing / spinning
the eyes seeing within themselves the knowing

deep & ancient, unconfirmed, undeniable
locked in skin
touching one to the other

there is
in disaster & terror
safety
      in storms of cold, in enormities of risk
in the black, the certain
human ugliness & death
there is
hope / prayer
praying for what is known
known to be real
touch of flesh & vision
feeding, feeding on
vision of flesh touching

nothing can deny the separateness of persons


by prayer / by hope / by what we call
love
love
by what we call love
prayer, hope, vision

hungry, the flesh
nourishes
      terrified
the flesh
comforts
      in need
the flesh
offers

open, the flow
open, the knowledge & the vision
open, the song, the touching / a commitment
to be

to be known
to be joined
one flesh

        be it remembered
        all prayers, all love
        all touching, all vision
        is Her holy gift


## UNTITLED


poets of the world, be
        careful.  i can't say it
strongly
enuf.  i know
i know
i tell you i know
that she stands on every street corner  waiting & watching
that she looks into the dark doorways & empty windows seeking
that she tirelessly walks up & down the hard streets of our world calling

      watch out, you fools.  you are blind
as well as deaf.  that's one of the things she hates.
be careful, poets.
its not enuf
to put a pretty word
next to another one.
a real image or two
studding yr verse
wont save you at this reckoning.
this is the real
thing.   take
cover, poets.
she is knocking on the door
are you shivering in yr shit filled shoes?
have you roses growing out of yr nostrils?
she is coming

she is coming
she is coming thru the door
she is coming up the stairs
she is opening the doors of the bedrooms & the eyes, looking in
she wants to hear no storys
she wants to hear no songs.
i think she's had her belly full of singing.


she is merciless.
she knows what you have done
there is no use crying abt it, making up fancy tales
you've gotten too good at that
anyway.
        she'll take it back.   it's hers.   she wants it back.
run poets,  run.
hide, poets,  hide.
be careful
take cover
i warn you
i know.    i tell you,  this i know.
she's coming.  up & down the streets, in & out of the houses, in the
        dark & the lite, seeking, looking, crying, mercilessly
        examining every soul.
i warn you
she is as relentless as you wd expect her
to be.
it's hers.   you know it.   when she finds you
she will take it back.

*UNTITLED*

trees are structures, like
ladders
      angel & man fighting, making it
      their hair & sweat
      that hangs down
      so green & clean & red ripe

five branches
against a sky
invite

      to the climb / a closer
                walk
        with
             the flower, or
                  bud

with its thousand points
of impossibly perfect
           stars


*UNTITLED*

no one knows
how to wait for the poem. that's
the thing. no one.

all waiting may be
the same, death
is waiting for us, we
wait for it. a simple observation.

if a man cd
wait
the poem, wait
inert & open, I wd
count that a major
craft achievement.

bench, beach, bed, any empty
space can be
so filled
if only one knew
know how to

## UNTITLED

the moonwash sea
is a storehouse of stink
ocean life
     sewer smell
       vomit
of a million cities silent
corpses churning
beneath the silver lace veiled face
crouched in the dark, we three
the total black punched
with torn star holes, broken
by slabs of
moonjag silver

on the wet hardpacked belly of sand
we squatted, three blooded brothers

we stared
at the sea & moon.   clawed
furrows into the sand.
smoked.

               i thot:              the sea as
mother, the sea as
woman / "o let me hear my brother's voice"
               the sea as saviour
the reservoir of love  /  "o let me hear my brother's hands"
i did not shout.
i folded my mouth & my eyes quite small
neat pack fits in
pocket

still we crouched
together, were
flesh of flesh, bone of bone
                              the best
we cd do.  the sea so huge

distance, also, we
shared.  not as
space, but as
a snake sucks
an egg.  goes at it so
careful not to smash
& lose.


UNTITLED


think of yr body
as a bridge
as it arches under & around mine

across which travel all passions & desires
from the back of skull
safely bridging the desperate cries

its structure strong & flexible
for the wind
& for the proper movements
of its functions

yr body as a bridge
a bridge to
my body as a bridge
a bridge to
yr body as a bridge


BOPLICITY*


miles &
        miles
for a
        to hold that much cool
water water water
        when I'm thirsty
plenty of ice cold
        when I'm dry
when I die

* Titled "Bopology" in some manuscripts.

# BLUES FOR BILLIE HOLIDAY

1.

soft & quiet are the rooms in which
the lady of day chants her runes & riffs.
reverence & peace to the sound.

an anguish ended. call
it a life. a lonely bed, probed, defiled,
too frightened to take her last fix.

the singer of songs, stilled.
the beautiful throat, clogged.
the hottest flesh, chilled.

2.

life is that disease
we are infected with at birth.
we die of it with ease
& become earth.

the earth does not care
about the body's scars.
to it all is air,
& stars.

o earth, our mother, enfold
this twisted & beautiful soul.
let her become a bird, or a tree.
let her be one with thee.

3.

mirror, mirror, in my soul
who is the guiltiest of all?
mirror, mirror, in my eye,
where does peace & penance lie?
mirror, mirror, in my flesh
whose name is written across the glass?

      man /
             giant numbskull dingo junkie slob
             angel killer cesspool bone & blood
             bird ocean moon fire earth knife
             skin torn death born eyes scorn jazz horn life

             o Goddess, grant him
             o poets, chant him
             o demons, taunt him
             o love, haunt him


4.

billie dead
in a cold bed.
paid up dues
no more blues

now she flies
thru the eyes
touches each face
in close embrace

she can sing
anything.
she can rest
has passed the test

you & i
have yet to die.
while she flies
we live more lies.

the lady sings
of truth & sorrow
the lady of day
the lady of tomorrow


# BIRD
*an elegy for Charles Parker, musician*


bird
frenetic dancer
weaving out of the darkness between the buildings
blowing high & screaming in

his arms dripped blood
his mouth, too, man
& his eyes

singing singing
bird of horn & bloody arm
how many sweet lips sucked that cock
& left it still frenzied & in need
to blow its own self
thru those fingers on that metal

they relaxed him at camarillo
& let him out
but he did not cool

leaped from the roof of his head
into the street of sounds
impaled himself upon the dirty spikes of gold
screamed his screams as the people danced
died

     what abt that horror, man
     what abt that pain?
     what abt that cat like all the time trying to do
                     himself in
     lushing / hypeing / insane fucking
     no sleep no eat just blow blow blow
     farther & farther out
     tearing finger from hand
     tearing eye from skull
     tearing sound from throat
     leaving bleeding chunks of bird caught in the teeth
              of many sessions
     what abt that?

out of his own dark skull, bird had to find roads
crawling on his black belly, his face ground in dirt & blood
broken steel splinters shattering his arms & his eyes
limp backed & half alive with his own death
he traveled his own way
made it
there
to the sound

& flew back in, blowing his crazy eyes
shifting & dazzling & laffing bloodclots down his mouth
out the window & up to the moon & into the cellar &
                        onto the bed
laffing & dancing & coughing life & screams all the way

like / when he cdnt fly any more
he fell down
& died

163

but he'd been there, man
& he blew

& he flew, man
like
high

  god rest his soul



## PORTRAIT


my friend is insane.
wild with words & love
he flows constantly.
people are disturbed by it.
  as he says.
      "clarion call.
  our poet laureate is in the madhouse."

charley newman has sad eyes.
he looks into his sad eyes
& sees a mixer of cement
grinding & crushing
its horrible noises grabbing
at the child's brain
while he sleeps.

he riffs in the voice
of a hurt child
& he sees things.

the concrete mixer that makes the obscene noises
he pours himself into

trapped with the rest of us
in the dead street car

blood filling his armpits & his mouth
he does not despair
but strikes at the hinges & padlocks
with hard blows of love


## *UNTITLED*


a plea to the goddess to implement this
curse on those who cuckold me

give them the axe
give them the axe
give them the axe the axe the axe

break their backs
break their backs
break their backs
break their backs

stuff them in cracks
pack them in sacks
stretch them on racks
tie them to the tracks

bind them in flax
burn them in stacks
boil them in wax
pierce them with tacks

burst their skulls
slice their skins
feed the gulls
from the bone bins

## UNTITLED

like ocean flowers
our brief sweet hours
as each unfolds
its center holds
stamen & pistle
of love, nestled.
the waves explode
make white the road
down which our dance
flies like a lance.
strait, brief, hard, sharp,
brite, gleaming, straight, true.

## *UNTITLED*

peace peace
we too shall
rest.

& in the air
                no breath
& in the eye
                no birds
& in the black
                no needs

then when we are nothing & one
& our flesh is eaten
by trees that thrust to the sun
& our blood is drunk
by lizards with flickering tongues
& all that we are is nothing
& all
& being born.

then over the fields of quiet wheat
the wind will caress
& there will be peace
& we too
shall rest.

*Love Is the Silence: Poems 1948-1974*

*This selection of Perkoff's poems is not meant to be definitive but, along with his* Alphabet *poems, to constitute a significant presentation of his published work. Shortly before his death, Perkoff and I outlined the scope of this volume with the explicit purpose that this book and* Alphabet *would form his selected poems. It was understood that I would choose from published books, broadsides and magazines indicated by Perkoff. Unfortunately, his condition degenerated very quickly and, before I could return with a selection, Perkoff had died. In every sense of the word, this is a posthumous volume. No claim is made to the authority of the selection outside the editor's appreciation and understanding of the poet's work. Certainly, this is not an attempt to promulgate literary legends or to preserve the already worm-eaten corpse of Venice West and the beat generation. There are countless testimonies as to the number of "great poems" lost or misplaced during Perkoff's rather erratic career but I leave other, more interested and personally qualified parties to track this material down. Enough, I think, of Perkoff's talent was sacrificed to fantasy.*

—Paul Vangelisti

# FEASTS OF DEATH, FEASTS OF LOVE

I

1.

down the Wolf River
backs to the sun thru water shallow & flat
beautiful girls & boys
      the birds wing tip to tip
      swinging thru & around
      calling, calling

we carried city eyes
over the rushing water
the stunned vision of scene after changing
scene
expanding & including
as our shouts & grunts & songs
wailed outward

    (I had to get out, once, & push the canoe from behind, my
body from the ankles up was hot, sweaty, sun gleaming, my
feet cool in the river, lifting & pushing the heavy canoe.

    I thought the others wd get too far ahead, & we wd be lost,
off in the Wisconsin woods, where there were neither Jews nor
cities, a world hot & in winter my feet wd be like encased in
the cement of the river, & the canoe wd never be pushed over
the flat scrapey sand.)

the river movement
coiled around our eyes
the quiet sound of the breathing of work
set the beat
of our songs

2.

The next year we took a different trip, out Lake Tomahawk
& an adjacent lake, I don't remember which one. In that part
of Wisconsin the lakes lay on the land like a thousand eyes,
peering into & thru each other.

from lake to lake
between two mountains
all blue green quiet movement water
in the air & eye
the huge walls rising
a great grass field
covered the inlet
& the canoes went thru
as over land, it looked
so quiet
  rustling of grass
    the soft voices
      hot beautiful girls & boys
        hot beautiful summer day


II

1.

wake up! to a morning
sun shining thru even newspaper
headlines
sun on
men in sand wading thru
blood

        'Woe
          woe unto
            the bloody city of Litchfield'
           he cried
        with his bare feet
        in the gutters of blood

naked feet
naked legs
naked eyes

    into the market place howling
    along the streets howling
    in the living room
         howling

the sun! shining  shining
in our eyes


2.


at the edge of the water
the glass house eye of God
embraced us, pure
in white

   clean after communal showers
& communal food


'Boruch ataw Adonai
Elohenu melech ha'olam
ha'motzi lechem
min ha'awritz'

reverberating thru the food
the eyes
the air out out into many rhythms
& tongues

sitting on the benches, bodies warm & throats filled with
            joy & love

we offered worship
sitting warm to warm, eyes & skin touching, love flowing
we offered worship

                    we sang
& spoke languages & poems
offered worship & love
mixing the birds of passion & the swords of God
in our beautiful young eyes

It wd always be dark by the time the services were over. & secure, in the glass house, lit by the God that shined all our faces, the burning candles of love in our bodies, sharing the glow outward to trees & wind. & the younger kids went to their cabin while the older ones had a dance, & carried on love affairs & intrigues & political arguments until 11:30, when the boys walked the joyous road back to their portion of the camp, singing & shouting, clean & alive.

By the time the Saturday morning services were over, we were so full & whole that anything was possible.


3. *political song*

the people circle the room
coming together

the blood circles the body
coming together

the earth circles the sun
coming together

        hang on, man
        as it
        wobbles around

        hand to hand
        as it
        wobbles around

o living communities
men & women who love & are loved

o living bodies
men & women who love & are loved
O loving cities
men & women who live & are lived

     eat
       drink
         embrace
          each
            other
              inner
                face

## III

### 1.

I see clothes piled in great heaps
against gray sky
with the smoke & sun in the air
of human flesh
& in the pockets of those beasts
who wear my name
things of value jingle & clank
in those black pockets
teeth & eyes & skulls & skin
in those black pockets

        there are bodies
        naked
        not talking of love

        in their last waters
        naked
        not talking of love

naked hunger
naked hatred
naked minds

    howling in the crowded boxcars
    howling in the dark barracks
    howling in the hot showers
    howling & whimpering in the final chambers

    silent in the furnaces


2.


such visions
wove their shroudeyes
thru our songs
such knowledge
blackened the edge
of every flame

each kiss
bittered with the salt
of their blood

   (Many summers later I hitchhiked over a thousand miles
back to the Wisconsin holy lakes, to speak anguish to a wise
man, seeking comfort, seeking peace.

   & we sat outside under a fat moon, at the edge of an open
field of grass, scenes of love & myth echoing in my mind.

   I asked him why the six million had died. I thought some-
how, this man, an Aronin, descendant of the first & holiest
priests of Israel, humble seeker & generous fountain of love,
wd have an insight, a knowledge, a hope.

God's plan? If there had not been such blood & terror on his mouth, he wd have laughed. & told me he had no answer, no peace. & told me of the many nites & days he had fasted & prayed.

& found nothing?

found only hope that came from the realisation of the cleansing & purification of pain.

Whose? I, so young, so bitter, so needing an answer, sd, whose? good for their souls? or ours! so bitter, so young, such needs.)


even now
it is difficult for me to fix in my eyes
the image of
the God/Priest
lifting sin from the souls of the people
                    my soul, my sin

clothing these six million in my sins
& thrusting them in their foreign wrappings
into the flaming mouths of agony


IV

when the sun dies
many other suns will still flame

all things contain the seeds
of their own completion
all seeds contain the things
of their own destruction

the sun
makes a morning
bright descending on hooded eyes

the sun's morning
floods into the sands of war

    wake up
    hang on

coming together
coming together
coming together


# NO TRAVELERS DOWN THIS ROAD

no travelers down this road
i wonder who's next
not to mention the birds! they're singing so loudly
goodbye, hello, whichever
is correct
i've misplaced my schedule
does the bus stop here?

brothers & sisters
husbands & wives
stunned & bewildered, stumbling
over anything

why are we crying? why?
& why are the birds so thunderous?
has someone got the time?

not only the names
have been lost
        (tho the names
      have been lost)
            even
the desire for names
has been lost

if this is the wrong road
(surely this is the wrong road!)
which is the right one?
if this is not me
who am i?
am i you?


## IN MEMORIAM: GARY COOPER


coop because i know you
dont care i'll tell you
all my poems
are movies america electric blink blink blink
flashing neon zeon flics flickering
heros heros heros big as the bond clothing people
on broadway or heads on rush
more

hey, coop! whoa! hey! shitkicking toe
no more.
dead.
great clumps of
hollywood burned the day you were
shot down by a warped orgone ray
yet old man reich died in federal jail for inventing
cancer but they wdnt have called
him in for you anyway cancer is sure
all american way to go coop
small consolation
doped up dieing while those ugly i mean to say
rich
houses under that
now dirty sign on that dirty brown hill:
        H O L L Y W O O D
went to
flame

& you
just
went.   toe digging dirty sly
eyeing jean arthur

dirty old man
jockstrap kept yr crotch flat
when the injuns were going to
burn you had you hanging
flat crotch hot katy jurade cdnt touch
yr lonely official tick tock cock at the
railroad train of terror
                              pure loo—
king cockless all
the way you

recognize me the director?   my head turned
backwards   legs tucked
tight into my feet? i dont know why
bother now  y're dead
cancer eating your flesh like
a ranch breakfast flapjacks potatoes
bullets mimeographed scripts lots
of syrup eggs & no one puts
anything
in the coffee
whoa hi ho
makes me so jolly not just
the houses
burning burning burning
but the way you cancered so softly into
                    (did you gulp 'yup' just one more time?)
being dead is a
laugh, a big, tough (i'm laffing)
cowboy (i'm
laffing) you know
cant
die in bed while hollywood burns.
                                        you
come back spit the fires

180

dead swoop on all out
laws & horses while yodelling
the canterbury tales & i'll
give you a comeback
role in the 'kowboy pomes'

dont pay much, but
beats dieing.
maybe.
anyway, so
long, coop
yup!


## LOVE IS THE SILENCE


love is the silence out of which
woman speaks.  the female
country, the grieving country.

                    i stole
those images from a
wild girl's mouth.  i am a
witch.  i deal with
death.  she sd.  i
struggle against it.
the poem
is my struggle, i sd. a different
craft.


            tho once i hungered
where the two crafts cross
to take within my hands
that power
& heat it
at will.

her lips moved in the dark room.  blue with
kissing that cold thing.  woman is
silence, she sd.
a different craft.


## LETTER TO JACK HIRSCHMAN


jack, let's talk
abt
the streets. OK?  where
it's all
happening, right?

what do we want from them? not
more blood, no graduate courses
in human capabilities. dachau
was the streets. how many more
such roads
must we travel?

let's insist on vision
i will accept nothing less than miracles
all men are unhappy
camus sd
& everyone dies. a street
all share

perhaps it is a matter
of language
            the sage says: man
is the language of
god. what creature or monster
forms our world
in its mouth?

where we walk
we know the dangers. if
the choice is between the streets
& literature
there is no choice

maybe we shd be talking
abt "joy". is that what you mean
by "streets" jack?

Poems Published in Magazines and Broadsides

## ON THE RE-NAMING OF THINGS

If I were God & had a
choice of all the names I wd
change these:
    children to laughter
    love to laughter
    & other things I wd
rename poem & little & clean
I think I wd then
summon all my powers
& name the poet Death&Beauty
& watch the world shrivel

## IF EVERYTHING RETURNS

*if everything returns to one, what does one return to?*
         —zen ko-an

the face in the mirror of
the human face
looks out on my face.    the eyes.

the hands in the mirror of
the human hands
reach out for my hands.   the touch.

the pain in the mirror of
the human pain
strikes out to my pain.   the love.

the people
present, the particular
circumstances of his being
there, then

the works, the sermons
the falling three times
under the cross

all these things
naked nailed
flesh by bone by blood by thigh
by heart by tongue by shattered eye
to the wood
a man, naked, screaming, hanging there, only
not
screaming.

    did what he knew only
he cd.
    he stayed
there

it hurt, it really
hurt, his hands
hurt & his feet
his whole flesh was real
pain

& he was thirsty.

         the salt in the mirror of
         the human eye
         burns at my eye.         the face.

         the wounds in the mirror of
         the human hand
         bleed from my hand.         the touch.

         the nails in the mirror of
         the human love
         tear thru my love.         the pain.

the Christian philo
sophist
in the white cold morning
sd:
    "even God
        (& he, Christian, believed
        that entity was
        & is
        an entity)
                cannot
        open & shut
        a door
        simultaneously"

the iconclaster
younger & of an older tribe
           (& he, not believing)
                    sd:
"making the natural laws
surely he took consideration
& kept a small secret
of his own"

continuity
continuity
is activity of all activity
opens & closes indiscriminately
all doors unconfused by

        direction

      (not a place, or movement

2.

"we step & do not step
into the same rivers"
sd another lover.

all things become straight lines /
the
oneness of them
the
allness of them

the flowers are withering / shall they wither?
the leaves are falling / shall they fall?
the clock is moving / shall it move?
the dark
is gathering.  shall it gather?

everything
a rhythm to it
ends

washing & rewashing
in the water

3.

the river was warm, but not warm enough.
the woman was beautiful, but an egyptian.
the child was hidden, but exposed.

the river gave up the child
to the woman
the woman gave up the child
to the king
the king gave up the child
to the wise man
the wise man gave up the child
to the angel

the angel gave up the child
to the people
the people gave up the child
to the mountian
the mountain gave up the child
to the Lord
the Lord gave up the child
to death

        to lovers of straight lines
        these are straight lines


4.

continuity
continuity
    (the action of activity
     the rhythm
     the structure

immersed & not immersed
in the waters
all things & people travel the long roads
from what is known as /
ending

        a dimly perceived
        infinite extension of the line


## ALL IS QUIET


        All is quiet now. They return
        to lives which they find
            filled
        with hate. They build
        their houses on the stained foam

of life they've killed.
They are sharply skilled
in art of death,
which is man's art alone.

Is there, somewhere, one
who dreams of love
and not of hate?
Who, with the fresh sun,
embraces wonder? Sings of
confidence to fight the fate
the modern world
has decreed to be ours:
the fate of cultivating
tears for flowers?


## A SMALL DROP OF BLOOD


A small drop of blood lies wearily on the window sill
Little green scum swarms in its midst.

Pubic noises scream their raucous tears of alcohol,
while man and woman and man and woman weep.
                                        Weep and die

and weep and scream and laugh in terror of my long
white brain reaching towards their souls.

Behind a door a baby dies. Its mother
gently masturbates to the sound of blood,
and the world drinks in the delicately constructed
orgasm. Death sneaks in through the keyhole of

my poet's eye.

It is time all small people returned to the grave,
yet the small drop of blood will not flow.

It sits quietly on the ledge outside the window . . .
waiting.


ECHOES, ECHOES

*the poet is the world's remembrancer*
—Lawrence Lipton


Children play among the roots of unkempt trees.

Stones that once were shrines are formed into houses of terror.

There are crowds everywhere, clustered & clotted along the sides of the huge buildings, massing quietly in the streets. They turn their impassive faces towards the sky, their eyes empty of color & love, their mouths set & rigid, their scrubbed skins glistening in the pale sunlight.

No heads turn. None seek to look upon, speak to, any others. There is an absence of warmth.

But quietly, seemingly unheeded, a whisper travels its course slowly through the crowds, speaking over & over to the unmoving faces:


"There was once a day set aside
for spitting on the king."

# UNTITLED

Take that everything's wrong, now,
& no one knows why
                              but two guys
arguing, one had the clue, Get
hip, man, to yourself

He sd.  & there it is,
(we, not seeing it, but knowing

Get hip'man, to yourself, the one
cat sd,

                    (not now speaking of rime,
altho its problems
                         sick-
ness being too much of a word, for this
          very similar

Man, to yourself
there it is, in you, more than you can touch

pick up on it like a horn, man, & blow
it'll swing you along
inside you it lays naked and evil
it's waiting to be born

                         Get hip, Man, get with it
before
it gets with you.

## THE RECLUSES

They paper the walls of their world
with their strange rhythms, visions.
They have within their deepest eardooms
fragments of freshest wildness.

              That of a woman
never feeling breastingly through their eyes,
they have no sin. But on their walls
of rhythmed visioned scenes
they often have lines about a mountain.

That black which is the greedy of the mind,
that reaches up and grasps from
the perceiving eye
all of the memoric stanzas brought on by the world
is their fine house.

They live there.
They have their own dark lines.
they are always

inside.

## TO ORPHEUS

      went down there, o
      singer, went down there, o
      luteman

      to where
      they dont dig song or
      singers

showed you knew who to
believe. climbing down those walls. hugging
yr horn.

& after, after the
stoning & that
scene

    to float the head down the ocean
    spouting trade secrets
    to lesbians

that was a cool touch


# THE SWING


up in san francisco, dig, he sd /
                   speaking then
of language
         ( a concern that
     occupies our needs
        currently

newness
in the word
the structure, like they say
or
in the swing of a line
a sound

using, he sd, the word in sentences
as brake up the flow of thinking /
   up in san francisco, dig, you dig
to shape the swing
to the tongue of a different eye

& I, thinking of the word,
                like,
as used to destroy a reality
within a described scene

                this changed line
of language, swung out
as we do it
                lines of thought
unknown
on the other side of the Grass

what might it not do, to verse, to thinking

an attempt, at any rate,
now carried on

POEM

hokusai called himself
        'an old man
                mad about drawing'

matisse died with a stick
strapped to his stiff
                        arm

drawing ten feet
                away
            (to purify the line, away
            from disease, from
            the crippled body
        how a line
cleaves
        how a line
opens, slices thru, lays bare

broken down to
essentials, like
a bone sticking white gleaming out

like
a slash-tongued bird
brite illuminating the air
thru which it sweeps

    up up
he straights his eye & wing
all background a blur of his holy speed
everything in the flight
the climb towards

      toward the
      eye, the
      central eye, the
      third eye, the outer
      eye

        'mad about
          drawing'


## PITHECANTHROPUS ERECTUS
*for Charles Mingus*


the unpainted shamans
of magic eyes
present their visions
for the tribe

*liberal academician*

o, pithecanthropus erectus

*1st hipster*

strange cat
to be the first up, off
the knees

*liberal academician*

standing there, strong

*2nd hipster*

the look
on his face. he dont know
what's happening

*liberal academician*

o noble beginner

*1st hipster*

strange, tho
to be the first up
off the knees

*liberal academician*

i embrace you for
yr courage
& yr terror

*2nd hipster*

at the same time
not even digging the
strangeness of it

*liberal academician*

we still in our time
feel it
facing the standing up
that you do now

*1st hipster*

maybe he does, man
there is some light
inside his eyes
              he looks like a
man, now, man
                the first up
off the knees


## POEMS FROM PRISON
*for Jana*


1)       *Dec. 29, '67*

in the dark, in the winter
flesh, closed as glass, surrounds its
hot core.

it is a battlefield.
winds bomb, cold erupts, pain
smashes against
the sanctuary.

yielding, it must not
shatter. holding, as it
feeds, is fed.

nothing can be
trusted, not memory, not
strength. only the
purity of the flame is constant.
the food, the feeding.


2)      *Jan. 18, '68*

soft words, silent words
dance in my lips
unspoken sing my flesh the vision
of touch, of touching

unmoving, all my body gestures
in intricate response to what
                    is known

deep, deep, beneath the bone
unknown calls vibrate forever
transformed as mirrors of joy
as joyously we reflect
each transformation other

in silence. in stillness.
all song. all movement.
in blindness. in pain.

all vision. all healing.
all knowing, all feeding
what we touch
as we touch

3)      *Feb. 7, '68*

the bird wing brushes close
to another's face
softening his vision to warmth, to home
to death in the flesh of his eyes
he sings! he sings! as i wd, as anyone
wd find that presence joyous
wd find joy

my throat is closed. my eyes admit
unlimited vastness of grey
& hard lite bulging them
into sharp edges

hunger is known to all, & need
but this, my pain, to me, my name, seems
                closer close
as the wing of song brushing
another's face


4)      *Feb. 15, '68*

i wd rather not sing
the images of my visions
thru which men stumble in clumps
bodys pounding unfeeling against
each other, against walls, fences closed
                doors

as tho the world built so huge
piece by uniquely structured piece
had been ripped from its balanced swing
                thru stars
smashed apart & gummed together
                tight & strained
then jammed into a tiny room
a dark room, room without air
to find its movements strangled rigid

rhythms locked & choking

all are moved inside this airless cage
not by memory of rhythm, not by desire
but only as great clumps of flesh might
                    twitch
in empty lust for quiet.  for the grave

what does not live cannot know death
what giant hand with master falseness
offers not even honest oblivion?

                    memory, memory,
move across my eyes,
that i may know the visions once
                    were real
a song, a touch, a total giving
each to each
one to one
one more song


5) THE HUMAN FLOW[*]
        *for Frank Rios*

the people are here because the machine is hungry
tho they know no more of this than do their guardians
not knowing, they must, as tho they knew
survive.  or not survive.  it is known some survive

                        (perhaps all are not equally appetizing
            where there are so many the machine need not be gluttonous)


[*] Also published as "Some Aspects of Prison" in *Love Is the Silence.*

the history of this crowd of food
is hidden
as are the histories of the priests, the words, the machine itself
but the machine has the solidity of its own structure
the continuity of their functioning contains the guardians
the humans in their rhythms feed, but do not remember

there is an immediate recognition of danger
no man knows, as he walks
who next will be stricken, blinded, maddened
minds are withered, bodies broken, souls plucked out
seemingly at malicious random

the disputes at this level
are not over names
but over theories of effective action

   if seven left leg limpers
   were spared under the half-moon
   while sixty-one others were devoured
   the left leg limpers acquire manna

there is a great body of such beliefs
all magical in intention
they permeate the herd like seasoning

& none are reliable. some survive.
cd he sing? more song appears. & then
the singers are taken

was he servile? the boots of the guardians
shine brite under the slobber tongues
then three out of four footsuckers are taken

was he repentant? comes forth numerous sinners, loudly wailing
& all the saved, the safe ones, are taken

most find they are forced to depend on
quick footwork, peripheral vision, alertness, an ear for the rhythms
they find little security.   most of them, also
the machine eats

in all its history of unbroken feeding
no portion of that flow has discovered
& passed on any awareness
of what they bring to that machine
the humans in their rhythms feed, but do not remember

not knowing they are machine-food
they blame the priests & guardians
who, not knowing they are only machine-feeders no matter what they name
    their rituals
blame the animals they herd

the machine knows no concern with definition
its only interest is that its needs be met
a constant flow of humans is ingested

## A SONG FOR MAX FINSTEIN

everywhere in the world people
are trying
to do it, to make, to make some real thing grow
out of their lives
into their lives

& each & all, singly
together doing
making
being
the best they know
how to
do

be
make
       real & alive

killers & haters & eaters of children
defilers, betrayers, the crushed & the decaying
they, too, must, i think
do their most real face
to their mirrors

if any, or all, singly
together, cd
know how to
had the magic of growth & wisdom
he, they, we
wd.   i wd.
wdnt you?


A CELEBRATION / FOR DOTTY / FOR CHLOE


woman at birthing holds
her holiest powers
direct from the source of all joy
all strength
she brings it forth / life
& a life
one & all, rock, tree, bird, man
eater & eaten, flowering
from this tiny
this perfect
this new
       formed bud
of purity

## SOME ASPECTS OF BEING A JUNKIE

*Come on! give me the medicines i need*
—Philip Lamantia

*for Fay Irving*


we plunge rituals of death beneath our skin.
skin / singular. as tho one. it is one.
the girl cried: "what are words? do they begin
to speak the act of touching, how it is done?"

"too many visuals" the poet sd
meaning our language. & our speech. & verse.
continuing (as tho it were not dead)
our gnawing at the craft. our joy. our curse.
"a vision is not sight, it is to know."

two different conversations, these. a third
illegal, silent, watching the blood flow
into the dropper.

          that there is no word
denies the need. this ritual condemns
human speech. & always present, the death
that forms the bitter root, the distorted stem
of plants that eat flesh. suck blood. throttle breath.
plants we call poems. or communication.
wasted attempts to speak, to tell by chance
what man cannot tell man. my craft now owns
no chant, music, invocational dance.
there is no thing clumsier than this cry
of one to one.
        from her:
               "i tried to die."
what words stab at, explode, destroy the eye
with that specific longing.  no. earth. sky.
woman. images passed from hand to hand.
but to have yearned to die, or yearned to yearn
cannot be passed.  flesh, its needs, its demands

is shareable.  the blood, untongued, can learn /
is brute / silent / deadly / red / neither poem
nor thought, but fact.  arm recognises arm.
veins recognise the needle slashing home.
the act ritualised, silent.  the act transformed.

perhaps it is my personal concern
to speak true, using words.  no words
break the flesh & cause the blood to burn.
this dance of blood is sd to prove us cowards
sd to destroy, to not speak one & one
to not speak touching, to end all desire.
but that sweet touch of death is flight, not run.
it is not running sets the blood on fire.
trees do not breathe with simple fragile breath.
the sea alternates choice of birth & death.
man finds his screams & poems & dreams are smashed.
man finds no speech.  man finds his touching crushed.

we embrace death silently.  silent the seed
the blood, the sharp needle medicinal
in concept / yes!  the medicines we need!
with speech denied, we try to touch.  & bleed.

## IN MEMORIAM: JANA PERKOFF 1944/1973

PRAYER

Lady, let it be
song, singing softly
in the darkness of my sorrow

1.

how shall i sing you, witch-woman, mysterious, essential
the fabric of yr being was woven

208

of such dazzling faces, costumes, dances
the names you named yrself
the tales, charades, histories & adventures
how?

sing softly the warm flesh so beloved
the physical beauty unmatched in my eye?
sing in my sorrow the wife, the lover
the lost, the betrayed & the betrayer?
how let it be sung?

what of the weeping, & the long cold nites?
what of the pain, & the unbreachable distance?


2.


i know you are dead
& i dont think i believe
the individual lives on as an entity
yet yr presence in my life is greater than it has been in years
i talk to you in my head. i know
you hear me

remember, i know
how to be with you when i am away from you
four years in prison
taught me. there
i talked more to you
than to the man
in the next cell

there i was suffering from crippling wounds
i felt only the warmth of yr touch cd heal
but we passed thru that
moved away from each other into separate lives
& then
when i saw you
& we touched
& all was peace between us, within us

the healing began
& you began to fade from the centers of my immediacies
but now you are back very strongly
& i know you want this poem in yr memory


3.

with you i entered uncountable realities
i put my head in yr hands & you filled it with visions
yr breath blew poems into my mouth
the goddess clothed Herself in yr flesh, for me
i climbed incantations to perfections of being
madness was a dance thru which you held my hand
traveling thru the debris of a constant flow stream movement creation
we hurt, used, manipulated, loved, gave, cheated, lied, laughed, held close
      tender
banging into, clambering over, getting around or thru in our rush
towards each other, towards the hope of love
the promises we gave each other & our selves
on a finger of stone extending into the sea
on the nite of our joining when you were wrapped in net & bells
then when we touched each other & knew it was real
the world burst into a cathedral of the white lite of revelation
& to say that the stones were jewelled & the sea was alive is to speak in
      commonplaces


4.

lost child, magical child
now you sleep, & yr fears are ended.
an emptiness is in the world & in my life
but always i have the songs which we sang together
the reality of yr closeness is imprinted on the bone of my soul
& all the gestures of yr dancing
move endlessly, forever
within the black mirrors
in the corridors of joy

# UNTITLED

1.

At summer's ending, leaves more graceful
than trees skim the wind to the
snow-belly warm, snow-belly womb. Yet I, flesh
hopeless of wings, clumsy my feet
to the fire. Birds
rise & soar / my face is
death, denies
song.

2.

My kind share the falling
dream / down, fast, not
as birds, but down down
to an earth naked toothed & knived, down
to be crushed, down, to die. birds
lift / settle / it is gentle.
I must wake to not-singing weight. Nothing
wings my substance, my solidity.

3.

Man's skills are enormous. The sanctuary
interplayed of lite & sound he cannot build. He
barely, only erratically, knows
it is. A gross thing
man, nurtured by chill soil, rotting.
Heavy, heavy with
hate, my hands move swiftly only to destroy
bones as delicate as the air
which beds them.
Burden of crumbling flesh,
heavy the stink of corruption.

I am a
man / have
no song


## ONE WAY IT IS

*for Paul H. Carlton*
*I speak, I speak because I must. But I do not listen.*


1.


I reverence words. The primary
act / to be
their functioning. It must
so be, it can be passed
hand to hand.

"Poets are all
liars." Words from Nietzsche's
head tilted towards secrets.
Saying also: "We
have art in order
to protect us from truth." Saying: "Poets
are all gossips." Secrets safe stashed
in his hairy lip.

All poets know
these are true. Yet, knowing, even
knowing, from behind the mask, after or before
the senseless violence, a poet
will sit in the sun's warmth, claiming
quiet, constructing
Rhyme. Such things have been found
effective walls.

2.

Graves are solemn
sanctuaries, tho not to
those whose hunger demands all flesh
be freed of corruption. They dream
a satisfaction. Carrion
dreams which calm no belly
spill milk in the streets, the famished
Beast will ignore the moist gatherings, the
intimate flesh.


3.

The driven ones: Berkman, Cassandra, Jeremiah / had
they three eyes? Children know safety
lies only in blindness. Kafka, holding this memory,
sought that dark. But he saw. Saw
the true way, that
it is actual, present, low & taut, so
placed to foil balance / that flesh may
fall, smash, shred, injure
cock & dignity.

Those forbidden explorations
cry: "Danger! Test the net." As tho
there is a net, as tho they too
need fear, need risk the stumble to
rot, to foul mockery.

Others / liars, gossipers, must walk
& wander. The journey remains. Wetly devouring
what they warm are, what they
wd be, they cannot
escape the leap as unavoidable
as death which waits with hand
extended, a constant. Waits
with frightened human patience.

The choice denied them, they face
what is. It is present, can
be used as temporary
fence or naked roof support.
What more safe than knowing, what
more secure? It
will be confronted.


4.


Is it madmen lunge to that
outstretched hand? To be
owned, choiceless, impelled / madness?
To know all
will be stripped to
decay & stench / madness?
They listen to their own
song. It is false. Watch their own
dance / madness?


5.


Vision, transformation, ecstasy of
serenity / these need
not to be taught. Are known
to the mumblers, cheats, deceivers, who
read / come close / lurch on. Is
it madness? There
are children.

# UNTITLED

1.

His destiny the inevitable
rot, man knows no renewal. Words
flower his mouth / distorted, deceptive,
they are buds.
He owns a hunger for
the infinite air, for those who
move thru it, mocking his destructive
gestures, his ponderous prison.

His reaching smashes, blinded. Twisted, weak, he
has not the fertility, the space of air. He clings
precarious to the vast naked surface
of his world / is boundaried
by flesh, has no escape
from its grossness. Clumsy, he yearns
for grace, for tenderness. As birds
have, as trees, flowers. They spring
from earth. Man is heavy, has weight.

Flesh is a cumbersome journey. Enclosed
in it, his screams are strangled. Betrayed.
That they are lies. In them, words
form the source, the core, his speaking. He
has collisions with all obstacles. He is surrounded
by walls. The inadequate desire, the
imbalance, the blurred eye / someone's
joke? He cannot laugh.

2.

These are human hands grip this pen.
It is my own thing, the man-thing, of which
I speak crippled records. By
my agony
I know my name.

As it is there for any man, thru me, flows
his total identity. All he has been, can be. All
he disastrously contains.
Man demands contempt, compassion, little
else. As all who are
man know, I know. Other things.
Only what is, is the Real.
The tomb of flesh is knowable.
A man's body is a map of history.
A woman's body is a map of history.
Brite blooms their fleshly intermingling, a
garden of
ignorance of decay which denies decay. The flesh
rooted, blossoming. Where
is anguish & corruption?

The myths speak of this
ecstasy. Speak of a later
complexity.

All are aware: from what
was came what is, came who we are.

What is / a growth
containing man's own being. A malicious
thing? Its structure
offers only words to say
its nature / they treacherous, totally
unreliable.

3.

To say true, we can say
nothing. Cannot say what is given
man to know.
some / with this knowledge / yet are compelled
to speak. As there are those obsessed with the structure
of the surface, seek
cavities, outgrowths, to grip
with the broken hand. That there be
then no danger.

The flaw is only their humanness. Hidden
& grasped to their handholds, even as they feel
out of danger
death greets them, costumed, belled. As
for a festivity.

but this eye, seeing
it vivid, undeniable / I will
never know
its blindnesses


A THANK YOU DITTY /
FOR THE CHICK
THAT FIRST TURNED ME ON


There is a country
    I don't know quite how far
        it is

            (but where I am
    man it can't be too far from here

the Grass really
grows

there
           natives stand in the sun
                 (not too hot, the sun

as I don't want
to offend yr sensibilities

& pick the pot /
              it
golden & ripe & already
filling the air
with fresh
        They pick it
        seed it, cure it, chop
        & toast it

the daughters
swing their lovely tits
over it
while they roll fat joints

after which
everybody there
comes down
& turns on

        Like I'll take you there
          I don't know quite how far
            this country is

where I am
it can't be too far
from here

*UNTITLED*

there will come a day
(poets will build this custom)
a day will come
with changes.
we cannot even consider them
without being thought mad.

    our caution
in disguising them as artistic
fools no one.
            (every rose pollinates.  even the stupidest
            know this)
no matter how beautiful
in the center of our roses

is the stink of
another thing.


*UNTITLED*

black burnt hills
touch snow at their backs

trees cry
& lay their whiplike arms along the ground

stark bushes
bleed red flowers onto cold wet earth

birds of shadow
　　　flying flying
on a hill of green
　　　as tho
long after us

　　　everything renewed
　　　& clean


# A BIRTHDAY POEM
# WITHOUT ANY NAME
# FOR THE NINETEENTH OF JUNE
# & SHE, NAMED THE SAME


1.

birthday
birthday
day of birth
eye of earth

earthday
mirthday
day of worth
weight of birth

　　　each day to each a god is born
　　　bless each wondrous natal morn


2.

suppose
(as a game
each day choose
its own name

she wont wear shoes
        lets call her 'foot'
her hair is loose
        lets call her 'slut'
she reads from books
        lets call her 'brain'
she swims in brooks
        lets call her 'rain'

she runs
she walks
she sees
she talks
she loves
she yawns
she moves
she dawns

she dances prances scorns romances
has songs to sing, has rhythming

she will not tame
nor be the same
nor force a name
upon the game


3.

goddess, in yr moontight gown
radiant thru the eyes, come down
among yr servants, worshippers
that she might see yr face as yrs & hers

& as one growing thing of clay, on the river bank
rooted in soil, growing to life, to know
that she is yr creature, flowering out of earth
as you are hers, in heavens where you give birth

each day morning bornday songday womanday earth
each dance morndance borndance songdance womandance birth

child mother sister wild
earth erupted, fruit & grain
bird
moon
ocean child
undefiled
goddess reign


4.

*to the gemini*

sons of the swan
yr blessings on
this child of earth
her birth & rebirth

like yrs, in her veins flows the blood
of beast & water, woman & god
god in magic waterbird form
woman of flesh & clay. sweet. warm.

holy breath
love & death
with eyes of flowers
under yr powers

as the sun is struck rigid in the sky
at precisely when there's no dark to the eye
when all is, as if by desire, transformed
from evil to good, from man to angel, from death unharmed

as these things happen
when all living breath is prayer
this moment of birth, in a transfixed world
offers earth love to heaven
as a lightning bolt
                    hurled.


5.


prayers to the goddess
prayers to the stars
prayers to the cake & the chocolate bars
prayers to the children
prayers to the game
prayers to the lovers
may each find his name
each day to each
a god is born

bless this wondrous
natal morn


### SCENARIO
*for David Meltzer*


poets in black jackets rush into the clock
time / arrested
busted
clock
stop!

the charge:
POSSESSION

        (but a hip lawyer
        gets him off

then the interviewers confuse
hunter & hunted
blocking pursuit, while

      bat-winged
the poets prowl the streets
anger & defeat swinging from their
empty hips
      seeking the lurker
in corners
      hoping to catch him
out, like they say

      going
      out
      after him, her, it, the whole
      gang

to put some
shape to it.

## SOME ASPECTS OF DISCOVERY
*for Tony Scibella*


1. *painting*

Lawrence called it
"making
 pictures"

& that draws my hand to it
the thing made
a bridge

to the eye


2. *color*

> *"only the black*
> *& the white*
> *have value*
> *color is a lie"*

why was it black & white
inside my head?
                now
that red blood pulses onto the picture

& that black

& white
the Goddess painted
then dances

        (a dream I have of
        pleasing her

3. *hands*

five pieces of flesh extend from flesh

what was the hatred?
                they had grasped my prick
                they had touched shit
                they were things people with brains didn't use
O beautiful hands
            taught now to pray
                        cut fingers where
the love pushed the knife too hard

now my hands dance thru the paint, & I want to smear it
    in my eyes my nostrils swallow it holy globs of
    color & lite

    bathe in the holy excreta of the soul!


4. *forms*

a round
a line
an intersection

                violent building
of the blinding line

*this is how it was /*
        He sd

"I will explode forms
how they land
will be man &
his world"

                it takes hands
                to set the thing straight
                so there can be peace


226

*UNTITLED*

kites & airplanes & birds
in a delicate sky

children etch laughter
on the still earth

the sun begins
its evening incantations

listen

the movement
of the sea

who walks with you
child of my eyes?

I can almost see
him


THREE SONGS FOR MY LADY

1.

be, my love, the goodness of yr flesh
& copper ripened richness be, yr hair.
be with the violent dancers of yr eyes
the structured house of vision be, yr face.

be, my love, that fragile mouth, yr cunt
a wildstreamed fountain be, my love, yr sex.
the poem of yr body be, its beat
& terror enclosing divinely, like sea.

2.

pretty pretty lady
o so sad you are
pretty pretty lady
wounds do sometimes scar

leaving on an object
imprints of a war
but these marks make it lovely
as lovely as you are


3.

love, love, o love, my wandering love
when shall I see you at home, at home?
you sing yr songs in foreign lands
while loneliness wracks my bones, my bones
while loneliness wracks my bones.

o come to my arms, & quiet their fever,
bring to their hunger yr warmth & yr flesh.
bring to my wintered heart spring, the wild lover,
resurrect my tombed eyes, my dry mouth kiss.

o love, o my love, my lost, lost love,
when shall I have you at home, at home?
sing no more verses in strange lands
while loneliness plucks at my bones, my bones
while loneliness plucks at my bones.

# EVENING

Soft, soft & quiet. Gently
the rigid hands release their hold
behind my eyes.  I rest.  I see.
I am empowered with visions.  I am old
& young, man & woman, child
& exploded egg wild
with conception.  & with death.
I breathe the air of all human breath.
I am touched with all men & all men I love.
I am all men, & I am loved.


# ON UNLOADING A BOXCAR

lifting
a piece
of black steel
& carefully

        (conforming to a pattern
            previously set down
            after extensive testing)

                placing it
on a construction
of boards
        extending
certain aspects of bodily structure
to the limits of tensions

            actions taken
        within a situation
                once calculated
        to destroy all pleasure
                now seem to contain
        evocations


## UNTITLED


o, fall, people, downward, past rock & shadow
as birds, outstretched & filled with love, do

    as they throw sharp & deadly weapons newly invent for the
    purpose of interrupting flight & ending the swing of the
    line of descent

fall, fall, fall
dissolve the tensions
that hold you to the earth

& risk
that graceful, formed ritual
outstretched, as the birds
& filled with love

# ROUND ABOUT MIDNITE
*—a poem for voices & music*
*for Charles Newman, Thelonious Monk, and Tony Scibella*


1. THE AUDITION

*hipsters*

dig
this poet
sits at a piano
clangling fingers against each other
bonkdblonk bonkbonk

listens for an answer
clagalingblonk
& listens

*dealer*

is he hip?
does he swing?
i've got dreams for his fingers

*hipsters*

he's been around before
at sessions up & down the street
always listening
trying to dig

*poet*

dreams i've got
who'll lay some fingers
on my hand?

*hipsters*

the sound is the thing, man

*poet*

if my left hand is dead
& my right hand is withered
& my arms are rigid
& my shoulders brittle
& my eyes are goofed
& my jaw hung up

tell me about the sound
like i listen
& hear what i can

*dealer*

you come on strong
like we dont know you

*hipsters*

who'd he blow with before?
who does he dig?
whats his story?
who is he?
does he swing?

*poet*

i've always blown
alone
in rooms & at the edge of everything

always alone in a circle of light
the words banging themselves out
into some sort of sound
& me, hanging on, trying to keep the beat

coming in once in a while
making it, not making it

me & the words alone in rooms
& at the edge

    *hipsters*

dig, man
he wants to come in

        what does he blow?
        what does he blow?

    *dealer*

down the street
not too far out
there's a chick

she digs wordmen, man
why dont you try to make it over there
& see if she can cool you

    *poet*

i'm hip she's the one for me
but sometimes it gets cold, man, cold
where i live
& i cant get warmth from any skin
& i cant get high from any kick
like my eyes are frozen to the ground
& my teeth are riveted together
& even the screams dont come out

thats when i remember the warm flame, man
the air thats more potent than pot
the climbing into the exploding sun
& falling

like down down
wailing

& she wont come in, man
shes as cold as my eyes

*hipsters*

hear him put the chick down
hear him lay hard sounds on her

*dealer*

man, the chick wails
with our band
all the time
if you cant swing with her
you wont swing with us

*hipsters*

we dont have no secret jive, man
we dont hold the keys to
                                    anybody's house
like we just blow

*dealer*

on this scene
all things swing together

*poet*

thats it, man
to swing together
let me come in & blow

*dealer*

its warm here
but everyone who comes in
has to close the door
or the cold winds stick up the valves
& we goof & shivver

man, that door wont close behind you
& i'm already getting cold

*poet*

where can i go
if i cant come in here?
where will i be when i leave?
i'm cold & awkward
but i know theres a high place
where everything swings
i've made it to the door before

*dealer*

if you make it, man
we'll see you again
& then we'll blow

*hipsters*

you come on so strong, man
pushing pushing

    dont blow too hard
    the reed splits

the sound gets harsh & ugly
no man can blow with you

    in those rooms where
    you've been hassling the word

sit & dig
sit & dig

you cant come in at first chair, man
come in in front

listening
digging

*poet*

the screams, man
the splinters & fragments

*dealer*

whatever the scene
whatever the sound

*poet*

it never stops
the screams, the fragments

*hipsters*

if thats the sound
if thats the scene

if the needle sticks
if the house falls in

sit & dig
sit & dig

*dealer*

there will be time
in yr broken cell
when the ice will melt
& the beat begin to pound

*hipsters*

listening
digging

*dealer*

but if the cat who wrote the book
has it in for you
& you never get to solo
& you have to sit up there & make that drone drone
& never get to blow

then dig that drone, man
thats yr sound

& dig that silence, man
thats yr sound

& maybe we'll blow together, man
later

*poet*

maybe
later

## 2. THE COMING IN

*hipsters*

dig
the poet

    he's been around before
    up & down
    trying to dig

    *dealer*

are you hip?
do you swing?
what have you got stashed in yr fingers?

    *poet*

my hands, man

    *hipsters*

is yr left hand dead
is yr right hand withered?

      are yr arms rigid?
      yr shoulders brittle?

are yr eyes goofed?
is yr jaw hung up?

    *poet*

the sound is the thing, man

    *dealer*

tell us about
the sound, man

*poet*

like i listen
& hear what i can
& if there's no sound
then thats the sound

*hipsters*

even in the spaces
between the grooves?

*poet*

then thats the sound

*dealer*

even when the screams are blasting at yr eyes
& nothing comes from between the teeth?
even when the blood banging yr eyes
isnt enough to thaw their agony?
even when it's cold?

*poet*

then thats the scene

*hipsters*

come in, man, close the door
before the chill does us in

## 3. OPENING RIFFS

*poet*

we come on quiet
man
moving down the street

*hipsters*

loaded
loaded with misery

*poet*

like we dont see each other
man
as we pass & touch

*hipsters*

loaded
loaded with misery

*poet*

we shuck each other about love
man
& tell terrible lies

*hipsters*

by not looking at the eyes
man
we invite disaster

*poet*

loaded
with misery
& cold

   *dealer*

who comes in
at the sound
"man"?

   *poet*

every man is man

   *dealer*

& who are you, man?

   *poet*

like
every man
is man

   *dealer*

what's yr story, man?

   *poet*

i leaped from a steel jawed womb
    to steel jawed breasts
& banged my childhood eyes on steel mirrors
great steel mountains blocked the sun i played in
great steel beasts destroyed many of my playmates

i crept thru the hard bowels of the metal monsters
    into adulthood

&  all along the way i tried to make music from the
    whimperings of
                        lost children who wandered there

*hipsters*

have you heard the howling in the nite?
have you heard the bodies twisting on tortured beds?
have you seen the faces of the children?
have you dug their sounds, how they dont swing,
    how they come on
                        so rigid, so square?
*poet*

that's the scene, man
i listened to it
i dug it
&  i dig it

*(they move into the 2nd chorus & the break)*

*hipsters*

the city streets
of hard
like sharp things
punching the eyes as they are walked
&  black
with dirt &  blood

*dealer*

seeming the death of all human rhythms
horns &  thorns
blasting all eyes eyes
until there are no earth spots
for feet to grasp
to communicate

*hipsters*

they have their rhythm
they have their drums
they have their songs

*dealer & hipsters*

throbbing the head
with bloodfilled eyes

    expanding ecstasy wombed
    in the soul
until it threatens
to explode the boned skull

*poet*

they have their magic
& their gods
somehow breaking thru
the crusted earth
somehow once again
filling the air
with fresh

*dealer*

somehow once again
singing swinging singing

*hipsters*

wild & wail
the inner voice
the nail
in the arm
the choice
on the sword

the child
singing in the dark

    level
       a
         wham
da bop!

     *dealer*

eyes!
man!
eyes!
is!
the!
thing!

     *hipsters*

eyes, desires
like they say

    we see each other with our needs & loves
    like they say

like they say
eyes

     *dealer*

eyes, man
eyes
   is
the thing

## 4. THE TURNING ON

*hipsters*

here she comes
the chick that swings us all

*dealer*

the session can begin

*hipster*

here she comes
the chick from far out
she comes on strong

*dealer*

three times hip
what she touches
wails

*poet*

man, she knocks me out
how many times i've stood in long lines in the rain
only to find the session over
before i arrived

*dealer*

he has eyes to be hip
he has eyes to blow
he has eyes to be cool

*chick*

some eyes are flecked
& twisted
move in pain, have no focus

*hipsters*

he has eyes
to be hip

*chick*

some eyes are clear, strong
move gently over the scene
move gently over the body

*hipsters*

he has eyes
to blow

*chick*

there are glass eyes
shuck eyes
eyes that try to put you on

*hipsters*

he has eyes
to be cool

*chick*

there is a high mountain
cats that have eyes to blow, to be cool
make it up to the top
it's my scene there
things happen up there, man

*hipsters*

if she digs you
you will come down wailing
if she doesnt
she'll flip you out
or push you off

*dealer*

it's a high hill
to drop down shrieking means
the end, man

*hipsters*

if you make it, & she digs you
& you come down blowing yr own true sound
then every wail will swing on that climb
from then on
every solo is blown
with one foot over the edge

*dealer*

sometimes she digs to come up quietly from behind
& at the outest moment
a quick shove

*chick*

things happen up there, man

*poet*

i've sat in this long
i cant split now
let's make it

## 5. FINAL RIFFS: FOR FULL ENSEMBLE

*hipsters*

the time has come
the page is blank
marked "solo"

*dealer*

& like all solos
a duet
if she will sing along

*hipsters*

some come on mumbling
dull eyed
goofed forever

    others come screaming down,
        their mouths twisted & gibberished
    their eyes burning themselves out

*dealer*

dig
the poet comes
once again

*hipsters*

man, they walk hand in hand
swinging

    their faces polished & gleaming,
    horns for the front line,
        upraised, to blow

*poet*

soft
soft & quiet
the rigid hands release their hold
behind my eyes
i am old & young, man & woman
child & exploded egg
wild with conception
& with death
i breathe the air of all human breath
i am touched by all men, & all men i love
i am all men
i am loved

*dealer*

eyes
eyes is the thing

*hipsters*

& blowing!  one with all!

*chick*

then the fire that i tend
eats away the rotted structures
burns pure & holy thru the eye

*dealer*

in the swinging group
each sound has its own voice

*hipsters*

yet all have the one voice

*dealer*

like
make that climb
man
wail

    *poet*

every cat
his own sound
his own name

    *hipsters*

then the thing will rock with a beat wild & free
then the eyes will be named & open
then the wailing will really begin

       every sound
       its own true sound
       every voice
       its own true voice

    *dealer & chick*

yet all sounding the one voice

    *poet & hipsters, dealer & chick*

love

*The Venice Poems*

A Poem/Sequence

> *polis is*
> *eyes*
> —Olson, *maximus, letter six*

# THE VENICE POEMS

*The Venice Poems* represent a book-length and, with the exception of a small fragment, previously unpublished work that deals with Suzan Perkoff's psychotic break in the context of Stuart's reactions both to his wife's illness and to the rapid changes in his own world of dreams, Venice, California. *The Venice Poems* are famous within our family and among Stuart's friends, and many consider them among the best things he wrote.

Stuart's own comments about *The Venice Poems* have survived, and follow:

> "what i am trying to do, in *the venice poems* is to draw on all my memories and anguishes of suzan's flip period, the whole period of last summer, so unbelievably magic & meaningful for *so many people* around here.

> & i hope to utilise other scenes of madness & love, echoing off of, related to, the central (theme) of madness (suzan's) & perhaps even unrelated ones, except by strange bridges & tangents

> & tie these images somehow to the madness of the birth of the city ("*what hangs over a city, from its birth, what auras & signs?*")

> not only, i hope, the personal madness & visions of its founder, but the madness that was america around the turn of the century, the euphoria that precedes intense depression in the psychotic cycle, a euphoria filled with images of simplicity & balance, which extend far into space/time, as far as the conceptions go, infinitely ("*glory goodness wonder / gawd bless our ...*")

> somehow i hope to tie all together the images & feelings of the place, the place here, where we are, where actually, so much, so much unbelievable wonder has rocked our brite eyed skulls that it makes ya wonder, like they say, it really makes ya, as it were, wonder"

—Gerald T. Perkoff

# I

what a city is /
    a coming together, a
    meeting
           or market, a
    proximity

what a city is /
    a dream, a
    container of
           dreams, a
    structure

what a city is /
    a scene, a place
           a place to
    blow, to die, a
    limit &
    a tool


2.


Venice California is a city born
of a peculiar
madness

        made a million from it
dug canals & let in the sea
        gondoliers & songs
pink stucco archways
        sold land collected rents built
houses stores flashing diamond toys

venice at the pacific, american venice, brite, new, expensive, clean
grand canal, windward, westminster, clubhouse, harrison canal,
                          carrol canal
avenues of water &
    summer homes for the wealthy

one or two weeks for the teachers & merchants
a long ride on sunday afternoon for workers

a man's vision
looks down now from the post office w.p.a. mural
beard flanked by oilwells & ferris-wheel
burning eyes on
canals into streets, cars on them
canals with garbage & slatternly houses swimming in them
the dirty pink arches of windward avenue
chipped
       carved
              pissed on
black with vomit &
money

      (oilwell
         throbbing in his ear
made a million

a vision
a peculiar madness, an american madness, a
dream


3.
      what hangs over
      a city
      from its birth
      what auras & signs

debris & clots of dead moss
scum the surfaces of the canals of venice west
fish live in them
kids throw rocks

across a wooden bridge into a moon-hip world at nite
the silence shattered by the deep rituals of cricket & dog
the fish wings gently splat the water stillness with plopping sounds

the great white dancer/moon
up thru the shadow of the wood bridge
life behind the housefronts/ imminent/ pressing


    on the ocean front
    a long row of brite bluewhite burning eyes on tall stalks
    silvers and shimmers the eyes
    changes all blue to rich purple
    red to black
    eyes see silver brilliances flashing from
    ocean orange lites

    up from the ocean
        the fog
          comes

    jews on benches
    looking coney island brooklyn
                but briter colors, more
    flesh showing

across wooden bridges
along the water on broken cement & rock gullied stumbles

    step by step, up the ocean front walk
    towards the brite noises at the pier
    past houses & hotels, for old
    people
    children send them money, the state gives them
    a little
    they get along

the fish / up! winged
thru the silence / sound
flowering the quiet water

    past empty grocery stores
    yellow lit the old ones inside
    waiting/waiting

step by step upon the wide cement
the moon changes her faces
the sea reaches delicate white explosions to the ear
the small trams hum noisily & slowly back & forth

the moonbeat heartbeat swing of tides
subtle
    rhythm
canals make homage
to the sea
        their flowers
gently
sing the moondance
love
to unwalled houses

it is peaceful to walk, there, at nite
under the limitless black bloodlustre eye
to feel life pressing/pressing from the houses
to hear fish, dog, cricket, sing
to walk high & loveling into the exploded mirrors of sunrise
a man
a fish
a bird
a star
swinging on a golden thread
its orbit
    thru great
sunbrite
    caverns

      born in madness, vision
      a man dreaming glory / wealth
      auras, signs, over the city
      from birth

4.

spring & summer
months of magic

        from venice
        to new york
        a letter:

dear david/
        monday, july 9, 1956
suzan
desperate after
weeks of struggle with
what was a terrifying combination of

        numinous
        paranoid
        insightful

           pressures

& pressures

entered, with a glad relief
  &,
     (on my part also
prayer

the general hospital
psychiatric unit

where she is now
where i go to see her again today
where all my hope & agony are now entombed

there are explanations, as you must know
impossible
to make

a loss
             (if what is lost is, precisely
                            everything
                            that is /
                                    reality

is too much more than just the word
to investigate fully

                i was observer
                & involved participant
                in all aspects of it

what i wd like now
to recreate, is that role:
the onlooker of love.

but i cannot put down a chronology
of the events.

a beginning is a growing thing. "people"
says Olson, somewhere in the wild *maximus*
"dont change.  they only stand / more revealed."

possibly certain things in letters
over the past month
indicated happenings.

possibly certain things in letters
over the past years
indicated happenings.

possibly certain things in lives
over the past centuries
indicated happenings.

                inflated with the Divine Mother
reliving traumas of her births
                searching the wild beds & hatreds of the world
for her twin

                her strength
her unhad power

                david, david
the tears that flowed!
that there cd be such tears!

                there were too many things for her to see
                she cd not sort them out

into herself, & me, the world & time
                into space & history
                        she sent her eyes & vision

the warps & stones & enveloping structures
                she saw thru
                        or around

until she came to that point in her mind
                where they were of enormous size
                        & shapes completely without reference

& she sd: "hit me, feed me, rape me, touch me
                do something real to me, that I may know, touch, have
                        something real to hold to. i
                        must have something to
                        hold to."

there is only so much that can be accomplished
by love.
beginnings are growing things.
there came a boundary, & i against it
stunned all my sharpness.

there came that boundary
& i, exhausted
                had nothing more to give
& only saw insanity in her eyes
& in my own.

                    beyond that time
i can as yet record little.
on the level of simple fact
i can say
that she entered the hospital of her own desire
& has so strongly a need to be helped

                    (by them, her lifetime enemies, the doctors
                      their white coats terrifying her dreams
                    since childhood

that i accept it
& am aware that it is good
that she is there

but the tears, that have flowed.
david
david
that there cd be

such tears.


            o burning eyes on the post office wall
            o citybuilder, moneymaker, oilwell & fun-zone
            at the playground at the foot of yr city
            the women drive each other mad
            their children hang limp & screaming from the pleasure machines

            o builder of canals & real estate profits
            touched by eyes
            at the sea
            things happen

                    the fog
                    the lites
                    the people & stores

5.

a city

magic & meanings

the real has

many faces

II

venice in a time
of love
          of tearing &
lost lost
following
          flowing the tide
back & forth
in & out

          venice in a time of love, of hate
of distance

          walks
up & down the ocean front
looking for
          calls it a trick
but
no trick to it
          just
                    "wd either of you
                    like
                    a blow job?"

the ocean is there
& sand for that purpose.

2.

yet some houses are looked to as
anchors
    to swing from & with them, their validity

in venice, in a time
        as any time can be

here they come
down the beach
two by two
three by three
down the beach
they come
carrying flutes & drums
saxaphones
pot
wine
poems

open arms & faces
        twisted
needs &
        loves

to swing
    the house & anchor
foundationless
    tottering on the hill


3.

in the car moving towards
chaos
    & joy
silent
it's silent
why is it so silent?

all that i hear are the sounds of the mechanisms
& the sounds of their flaws
& desires

watching no birds fly
from no mountains
poking in the dark
trying to find the intestines of small animals
no signs

it's ominously silent, so silent
the voices of their flaws, their desires

music
bodies
thunder of fucking & horns

each part separate
& unique
        how to prepare the
event?

        (with love
                in venice
                    in a time
                        of love


4.


to know the houses, that they crumble, that hills shift
with the movement
of the great swinging ball around the burning eye
that the canals flush themselves & are sea/ are
dirt/
        houses falling

but groping thru rubble, thru hatred
in venice
        in the love warped world

the many lost
driving thru the nite
walking up & down

        stone faces/ &
        twisted faces/ &
        hurt faces

here they come down the beach
wearing their needs & wounds
        like
great insects at their eyes

reaching
touching, sometimes

in venice
in a time
as any time


## III

trying
always
to
survive

against crushing jaws & walls
sweet poisoned dreams
glare & brilliance of electronic lies humming the brain
dark corners
        where children moulder

struggle is harsh
    makes people harsh
makes skins & hair
    coarse
keeps the bones of the children
    brittle

brings awareness of
pressures, of
proximity, of
            danger, of

                (sometimes

                            love

keeps a
cleanness to it, a

            distance

        I V

            glory goodness wonder
gawr bless our
    home
every day
in every way
better &
        those nig-
                graws
        those unenlightened
                swa-
                    vah-
                        jazz
we must
        they are
why
        my dear
like
        they dont wear
any
        clothes
                you dig?

                frightful.

267

hummy buzzy women in a cursing circle
        their ritual weaving & crossing, sewing
knitting flashing needled crotch covers for their own & other
        bodies

purity out of
        the purest

                o mothers, mother images!

                        vote gold
                        vote stability

hip hoo—
            raw!
        thou shalt not hang the cat up
        on money spikes

america in its brite gingham butcher jacket
america with its sunlit roads between insane asylums of houses

    (an idiot christ wandered thru its cities
     his face slopped in foolish smiles, shuffling along
     washing his palms in country wells

                                darkening
            them
                    saying /
                        "what's happening? what's happening?"
        & the people answered /
                        "everything fine, man.
                                everything fine."

o america
grabbed fistfuls of grandfathers
jammed them into the narrow corners of streets & factories
ran sewing machine needles thru their eyes
pinned them to
dim roachcrawled walls
broke their bones in the streets

gunned them down
            as they left
synagogue &
                poolhall

        o america
        great tree
        spreading foliage
                    starving the new growth
        extending probes to absorb
        water, life

                        dry root, dry leaf
        slender
        broken
        body
        crushed & bent into shapes that
        hurt, that
        scar the bark, the
        sweet sap
        soured & bitter

in the long dark lofts
        the flash of needles
in the quiet parlors
        the flash of needles
america in the early 1900's
        needles for the eyes
                (for the stretched tight
arm

hit me
    daddy, like
        fix me
            daddy, like
                jolt me
                    daddy, like
                        take me all the way
                                out!
                                    o america

269

                              needles flashing, whipping
                              over the face flesh of
                              america

out of
    cities

dreams shifting
to space &
ocean

            starving
            fighting

made it thru
        to
    here

            whichever face
            it
            wears

        (the place

                V

a city has
smells
        in the summer nite
along the beach or prowling the
glittering avenue
                              venice
stinks
a stale shit smell

old & rank

         fallopian pipes enormous belchers
         bleed into the sea
            tho they say
            the sewage dont
            come that way
            no more
            the smell, the smell comes from
                    somewhere

from the windows
of the strangled buildings
from the rotting mouths of the gapejawed
breathing in a little of that cool
air

      the moon over the bed of disease
      burns a brite blue
      She flowers dust upon the eyes of venice
      & the people are driven out into the street
      mad
      to drown their eyes anguish in burning fumes
      hurling themselves against
      the stucco falseface of windward avenue

              let me out, dear God
              let me out, let me out
              i been in here a long time dear God
              let me get me kill myself you God
              out
                  dear God

2.

one room.
a limited space.  a world.
madness & love absorbed in
the walls.

a safety.  knowing others
went from here.
returned.

       "o you who dig
          o we are all just
       dig me up again &
          frightened little children
       wolf me, wolf me"

one room.  five people
stepped off.  here.  five different
roads out.

       back is
       hard, a
       climb, rock
       strewn

       back is a
          killer
       like they say

          (been in here a long
                 long
              time

        out
        out
       out
        dear God


3.


not Venice's dirt, not windward & market street winos vomiting
   in the morning glare sun
but st louis, fourth street, south broadway, scenes of childhood
   & desire

three dirty blocks from riverfront
pressed in by warehouses & bitter men
a dark sign loomed: "erie house"

they sat on a balcony porch jutting out over south broadway like
   a bruised eye, looking down on those who'd had to sleep on the street,
   & on those who scuffled to work under their sagging bridge

as the day wrack on their ranks thinned, & the people hurrying home wd
   be stepping aside to avoid their morning watchers, hungryeyed, slack-
   faced, hands threateningly begging

by the time we arrived in the evening to go to the bar that was in the
   same building most of them wd be still hungrily lacerating  themselves
   before our horrified fat faces, begging for money & love, displaying
   all the wounds & infections of their ugly traditions, performing
   strange torn rituals of supplication & desire

it was called "little bohemia" & we went there often.  the owner
   was a young painter with a long slavic name & a beautiful wife.
   the fact that she wore no brassiere & that they were not really
   married was very important to us

as was the jukebox with its beethoven quartet & its political songs,
   as were the arguments the beer, the getting laid

i wrote poems there which aped patchen badly, & argued about love &
   trotsky with rotted eyed ex-stalinists lost somehow while
   waiting for the hammer to descend

in the daytime
i wd pass it on my lunch hour walks
hot ugly cement glaring
visible odors wetweeping up into the motionless air

inside the bar

      it always seemed cool

        a haven

on one such walk
i saw
a man picking in garbage cans for food.
i was seventeen years old.
i had never seen it before.

whatever it was he found
he stuffed it into his sack & hurried on
a man late for an appointment
pursued by his lateness

it was 1947
our hopes were high
the eerie houses & garbage of the world
were about to be destroyed

"the wall!  the wall!  the wall!" we shouted
  "bring it down
  "bring it down"

& in our visions of work & love
saw it destroyed
& the light once again
shining the corners of the faces

at nite
music
our growing desires
visions of touching & love

we knew the feel of the gun on the arm
the feel of the machine under the hand
the marching feet
the song sun burst processions of new & wonder filled faces, shouting
    psalms & offerings

yes!  then we danced in the streets
& knew love
yes!  then we sang praises & created
the wallless rooms

false gods
false gods

        but the fire burned
        & by its heat & light
        we watched & warmed our souls

false gods
false gods

        but the fire burned
        & the passion we derived from it
        impelled us, pushed us, drove us

false gods
false gods

        but the fire burned
        & the food it prepared
        nourished us, gave us power

the fire burned
burned
burned

& it devours even now
all, all burning things.
from our long  & intense knowing
of its flaming eye
we seek to walk unharmed

naked

open

in its radial center

4.

a city, a
prison, a
slum

     hard eyes
the children
pushed out on the sand
in the chill morning
hiding from their mothers in mud & hatred, burrowed
their eyes scummed, runny
their general blondness a
sick thing
a bloodlessness

facing these soulless creatures
one two three their parents march off into their violent wombs
scorching their eyeballs with lust
listlessly fucking each other, themselves, wives, sisters, children,
    anything, what the hell
anguished faces
laughing anguish
running from hiding place to hiding place
shrieking panic along

              the open street

    over the shoulder
         the frightened

                  the heart
          magnified

the eyes
  the eyes

(out
  out
  out
  out
  out

along the beach, up & down the canals
the blinded run in search of the blind
                 the cold
seek the warm, the dead
      the live

   & pass each other, blind
eyedust red & agony
into the factory, the grave, the hideous marriage bed

the ones who flame in a circle of love
as lost
as blinded
as fleeing, seeking


5.

stale smell
  burning flame
blind eyes
  love hunger

foundations & people, the venice strong houses
swaying in the wind

           pushed this way
         & the other


origins have
       shape, can be
touched, have
       faces

hands
    black
piano players
their voices, their
songs
        heard

thelonious sd/
            "eyes,
                man!
                    eyes.  mark the chalk of life
on yr eyes"

& bud powell sd/
        "in my arms
a thousand eyes

ten blind birds strike against
an ominous sky

the world is wandered endlessly by burning
black eyes

& terrible /
            the things they do
            the things i see
            the songs i sing

& terrible
& beautiful

my hands"

                great dark voices:

                    cripple clarence lofton
                    romeo nelson
                    montana taylor

                    speckled red
                    jelly roll morton
                    james yancey
                    bud powell
                    thelonious monk

all these &
    others, their
voices also
    heard, here

then thelonious spoke of his ancestry /

"stick pounds/the leg
stick pounds/the leg
feet strike/the earth
feet strike/the earth
eyes strike/the throat
eyes strike/the tongue

chants fly into the still time
flames eat great chunks of dark nite
feet move in ritual patterns

    bo-
        dies move
in rhythm

bodies
move"

& Jimmy Yancey took ten thousand fat fingers & sd/
            "if i can do this
            which cant be done
            then you can
                        love, can
        love"

all the voices
their stories
            some say
"yeah" some simply
                scream
chants & anguish &
eight beats
            sometimes


            88 keys or


88 million
            infinities of sound


fingers trying anything
breaking the thing
up
& pasting it with blood &
piano wire



2.


the salesmen's voices
also heard:
            "enter any time
the contest is just
                beginning


& it is impossible to break it
tear it
or stain its lustrous
                        transparency


the
  perfect
the
  only
the wall that walks with you
talks with you

eats sleeps drinks &
     well you can imagine
the rest

  yes sir! it is
removable
  but
who wd?

no madame it will not smear
yr face

come on
like
real

make sounds
like
open, like
love

get right up to the actual living
scene!
   ladies & gentlemen

all the excitements with none of the danger
they cant see it
you cant see it
but it's
there, it's
protecting you, y'r
safe
  absolutely

    & this is guaranteed

no
touching"

3.

over all
the Moon's soft singing
              blesses the hands, the wailers
wails with them
              blesses the torn, the anguished
moans with them
              blesses the salesmen, the shucks
crys for them


              voices heard
in venice
              hands that reach their snaketongue fingers
into the ears
              black hands &
              white


caressing
the houses



VII TO ABBOT KINNEY,
    THE FOUNDER OF VENICE


              isnt flying only how
              the eyes look, up
              or down?




the souls move into the regions of the clouds, the cloudless
                                air
they soar into the eye of the black clear nite
& some
sweeping thru, up, glittering their wings in the brite shine
                                of their golden faces
slip, fall, dont make it
clash down, clatter onto the hard

soil, or
catch themselves in sharp trees, dark
trees, tangle themselves
die
or lay there screaming

  their eyes still see the
  black lady
  ringed in brown & gold
  colors dancing round her at
  the darkest hour

  feel her breath on
  their faces, feel
  the warm triumph of her
  love, feel
  the sharp points of fear
  that jab them thru their torn & bloody flesh

didnt make it, dont make it, they are
mad & very
sick.
  they can
almost speak
but the star points of their bursting memories
behind their eyes
make their tales incoherent &
filled with mud &
    confusion, as venice
is, now, kinney, as the whole
world is.

even walking down the street
towards the sunset
thinking of nothing but the houses, how they are
against the sky
even then there was a woman beating
beating
beating
beating a child

thru a
window, in the evening !
even tho
the sun was shining!

thinking only of the houses
how they are
against the sky

        in oz books the houses are
faces, can talk, are alive.  along venice blvd
they soundlessly keen, as in a mourning

        good mourning, comrade
the committee is going
to kill you. joseph k. kkkkkkkk.  dada dances
on yr grave, singing
        haha
          dada.

        good mourning, blues
blues how do you do do do
             do me like a
tree, love, tall at
the funeral

        good mourning, mr zip zip zip
is my head cut as sharp & short &
jagged edged
        as yrs?

kinney, on yr streets
death's young musicians on their motorcycles
are reaching their sad faces out &
sadly
   o slowly how they
        falling falling

        & no one knows the
trouble on the scene

                three pound kilos you cant get
them kind no more.
                hardly.  hardly at all.
& then the fall.

        isnt flying only how
        the eyes look, up
        or down?

but looking down, past yr own
torn flesh, into
the mirc & knifelike pits of
the soul, that's a different story, when you
dont make it

isnt it
        kinney?


        VIII

        under the summer sky
        moonchip brite & godlike
        the ocean
                a woman
        walks.
        the fat of her
        flesh ugly
        overhanging her
        reeking the sweet perfume
        of alcohol & lust.

        in the hot nites
        the people come to venice from their cages
        come to nuzzle the soft breasts of the ocean
        to find a
        peace, or a
        frenzy, an escape, a
        road.

come to be healed, come to be saved
screaming & laughing
down the beach
strangling each other
devouring flesh & gnawing on
fingers broken & bones of
splintered fragments

laughing
falling
swimming
looking for
love, or their
souls, looking for a
fix, or for
death.

all these, crying, & i
cry
compassion in the name of
God, in the name of
the Mother
compassion for my
rotted stomach
tells me i am
befouled
my own wallowing, my own dark odors
climbing the insane ladder
into the ocean air.


2.

what is it eats at yr soul, man
that you kill?
what is it plucks at yr eyes, man
that you submit?
what is it stamps its bloodyfeet on yr children, man
that you accept?

men & women of venice, lovers, children, holy citizens of
                    the heavenly city
all around you there is the sweet air of love
breath of the Lord
soft kiss of life
touching yr lovely mouths

all around you is the peaceful black of rest
breath of the Lord
the infinite embrace of death
enveloping yr tender skin

you move at all times thru a garden of pure
ecstasy, all life pours
its fountains thru you

men & women of venice, all cities, the earth, the universe,
                    children, lovers, holy citizens of the heavenly
                    city
what is it
            eats yr souls
            plucks yr eyes
            stamps yr children
            turns yr faces
            away?


3.


the city itself, what it
is, a
city of walking at nite
city of old & ugly houses
city of real pain & real children
city of open sores & open eyes
city of doom & terror
city of ocean & animal lust
city of dying & strubble

city of venice, my city, city within a city i do not know or love
wondrous city, city of birth
city of water & air
city of fire & earth
city of venice, my city, doomed city, living city
city of magic, of stairs & ladders, of
roads.


4.

cry compassion for all
things, real
things that love &
touch the many
structures


our own wallowing, our own dark odors
climbing the insane ladder
into the ocean air.


## IX

what a city is /
    a vision, a
    holy eye, a
    structure

what a city is /
    a face, a face of
    love, of the place, the real
    place

some
cant take it, cant
look, cant
get the whole thing, see it real, naked
not the soul, especially

not
the eyes

      cant look but
only then
the growth, the magic
real
    the place
real
    the love
real
    is the place
is
    "bliss is actual
    as hard as
    stone"
      creeley says
the word
      is love, is touching, is
the place
      has many
real faces

        yes, there is a kind of
        knowing, it can be called
        love.

                *venice, california*
                *2. jul. 57 / 2. jul. 58*

Unpublished Poems from the 1950s

## UNTITLED

to move with the current of

moment, mindless-

        -ly, a

nijinskyed bird.

        restless, restless heart

beating

erratic rhythm, woman

rhythm

    in the

blind movement of

it.  heart restless beating.  mindless-

        -ly.


## A CHILD

he is in the

middle.  an axis, he

is.  it

revolves around.

even a war, or impossible

flight.  he takes it

in.  into himself.


ONE.  TWO.  THREE.

ten are the fingers.

twelve are the houses of the moon.


seven are the pathways thru the skull.

zero is zero.  it is.  itself.


the three pointed clock swings its timeless face

its hip ticking welds all numbers, signs.

   its sway twists the sound

         the blower blown.

one is the one & all.  one is the zero of walls.


all touch ten fingers to twelve moons to love.

## AT THE EDGE

Everything comes eventually

to break on this rock.  Or else to sink

within these depths.  Everything.

                      The melodrama

within the soul, the passions and long knives.

The joke extends beyond the centuries.


What an energy!  Pushing, fighting,

struggling, killing.  Then, suddenly—

Poof.  The waves swallow it.

                  They will say:

it is important to  :  it is vital  :  survival depends  :

   your brothers plead  :  the life of  :  never in history

has  :

      poof poof poof!


There are words, and words

                   production marriage loyalty

honor solidarity freedom love God

     There are words:  blood death

club gun kill screw live hate.


No flowers grow here.  A broken back,

a cigarette, a dirty thing containing half

of a million lives.

        The waves against the rocks.

The rocks against the waves.


If all the seas were one sea,

what a great womb that would be.

If all the seas were one sea,

what a great tomb that would be.


Only a few feet away

hundreds spend their hard earned Sunday

hitting their children.  Ogling girls.  Clutching breasts

and thighs.  Eating.  Sleeping.  Loudly screaming,

playing at play.  What a great

tomb and womb!

        Everything breaks on this rock.

Or else disappears into this mouth.

Everything.  Everything.

# AT THE EDGE

MORNING'S BIRDS
TOGETHER CLUMP.  HUDDLE.  THEY HAVE
SILENCE.  SILENCE.  THEY LEAN
TO, INTO
THE SAND.  KNOWN EARTH CLUTCHES
THEIR AMPLE BIRD FLESH FULL

MAN IS SLOW
TO MOVE.  HIS UNLIKELY
FEET THRUST / ABRASIVE SAND / NO YIELD / BURN CUT / TENDER FLESH

FROM CEMENT TO WATER TRAVELS
AN ANCIENT MAP
WHOSE BLIND CARTOGRAPHER SPLOTCHED
FULL-BELLIED BIRDS ON IT
PIGEON PIPER GULL EACH ITS
OWN LOOSE SEPARATION.
MUCH BIRDLESS SPACE ALONE EACH BIRD
ITS RESTING.
FEW WING-TUCKED HEADS AS A MAN
WALKS LIFT TO LITE.  TO MOVE.

THERE IS NO MAP WHERE
THE OCEAN IS
IT IS HIS HUGE, HIS MOTHER, HIS DEEPDARK, HIS FEAR
THE OCEAN DOES NOT KNOW HIS WORSHIP RITUALS
ITS RHYTHMS & FERTILITIES NO DESIRE DRIVEN SEEKING NOTHING ETERNAL
    MOVEMENT
AS HUNGER FLINGS RELENTLESS
BIRDS FROM BOUNDARIED MAP
INTO AN AIR INDIFFERENT TO
BIRD OR MAN OR WATER'S FLOW
AS MAN'S NOT MOVING EATS THE TASTELESS SUN.

sparrow fly, gull screech, owl hoot, birds of all colors & breeds
do what it is
you do that makes you
distinctive, i
love you


gull, dove, sandpiper, nameless scavengers of the beach that i see
each day as i go to pay worship to the
ocean, o birds, o
birds!
       there is no saying what you do, sweep, soar, dive, glide,
                                you are
beyond human
description, i
love you
birds


     & tony scibella
who is a man with two
eyes
   sd: 'you must have been a
                 bird, sometime'
& i dont even believe in rein-
-carnation, but i hope he's
right


sparrow, gull, owl, crow, hawk, jay, eagle, dove birds birds birds
myriads of feathers &
flying
eating what has to be eaten flying what has to be flown
i love
you, birds, i
love you.

## FOR DYLAN THOMAS

what'd
  you say yr name
was?
        & yr
            boy's name?

he was
        a
      (o yes, death, mr death
swinger
all right


## PAS DE DEUX
*A Dance In Counterpoint*


Carefully splitting centerwise,

apportioning experience equally

(if possible) I am surrounded

by things to which I belong.


On the side of the law:  wife, children, books,

Each morning's clamor to the world constructed

primarily of machinations and zooming combines.

On the side of the law

       the guilty fingers of childhood

the loves and heavy desires moving

       through the fingers

On the side of the law

       the forces of value and profit

the losses of forces, the forces of loss

       the law on the inside

on the side of the law on the

       outside


Much of the material of structure

and some of the structure itself

is here strongly caged, caging the

anarchic impulse, the deep rumble.


ii

       Everything contains

its own death.  Not only society dies by its own hand,

Within the shield of weighty decisions

the love breaks through,

Look, we have

come too!

        The night life moves into its

half of the room, and I am surrounded by

things to which I belong.

                On the side

        of the night:

wife, children, books.

Poems, the interspacing of beauty in love,

love.

        In the automobile

in the heavy smoke,

every inch of the blood

commands a new manifesto.

The hands that spend their days

grasping and counting,

stacking layer upon layer

cry out:   "five fingers

"are five roads."

The unsuccessful split

combines within itself.

        My careful dealing

of one to the left, one to the right,

one in the pocket, one on the floor—

                all to

            no avail.


I am come together.

        On the side of the night

        the law moves.

On the side of the law

the night envelops.


        Beginning again to chisel

at the cracks,

        carefully spending the coin

of the past,

        I am surrounded by things

to which I belong.

## UNTITLED

The women smell sweet in the city,
in the summertime, at night.

They open like nightblooming buds,
& freshen the air.

There are other things / flowers smell
good.  The air tangs from the cool sea.

There are times when it is sufficient
to make lists of things

to be thankful for /

that the night is dark

that there are flowers everywhere
that things have smell

It is possible to touch things.  With
the fingers.

## LETTER TO DAVID GROSSBLATT
### Concerning the disappearance of the "Two Musicians"

You started the painting,

then let it drop.  Why?

I saw the early forms, yellow and black

against the room,

moving from your eyes across

the fingered canvas,

the long horns raised, about to play.


But no sound.  And now

it is abstraction, stone or rock,

forms hard in structure,

dark, heavy rhythms.

I don't deny this new peculiar beauty,

but, those two musicians,

they almost started to play.

Hands to horns, breath in, jaw and lip

tightly prepared,

when one horn disappeared,

and then other.  Faces

followed.  In an afternoon, gone,

leaving only a faint memory

of their almost music.


Somewhere in this heavy canvas,

depth and hatred surrounding its

forms, the breath of music lies.

Perhaps, when all

is quieter within this rock,

the players will reappear,

stand strong upon the heavy shapes

to which they gave birth, and

play the yellow and black duet

of love you have

in your hands.


## CONCERNING CERTAIN TYPES OF WISDOM
*for Hilary Hultberg*

The young know.

The young know all the ugliness.

Age mellows the scarred mind,

false light of years looks back on pain,

& remembers beauty.


The young are near pain.

It looks in on them as they sleep,

& speaks of sick, dead loves,

& ugly waste, of emptiness within the hands.


Age remembers warmth in the bed,

& conversation based on private languages,

lovetalk, sweetened with smiles & soft caresses.

Only the young feel the cold hatred that passes

from heart to heart in the lonely night.

Only the young know the unspoken words,

the sick bitterness of the rigid body in the bed.


Only the young know, being near, being

in the hurt, being hurt by it as they breathe,

being struck again & again in their soft white faces.

No half-light of memory:

the glare of reality probes within their wounds.


I came to the world in a time of terror,

when men moved in horror-laced sleep

toward their single deaths.

Slowly across the streets they moved,

missing their deaths, seeking

their various deaths beyond the buildings,

reading it in books, newspapers.

The tabloids screamed:

"Outside! Outside! It is there!"

as tho to point to where it was,

& all moved as under water

following the finger, seeking it

beyond the docks & skyscrapers,

trying to manufacture it with

their small machines.

I came to the world in a time

of sleepy terror: an age of night,

a movement of half-awake dying things.

Only the young know.

Only the young know all the ugliness.

Only the young can speak of death.

## UNTITLED

english, the language  /
hard to speak of love
using it

not only that, one talks
to women, it becomes
another tongue.

it was different when
there were quests established:  either
you do or
not.
now it really is
foreign:  i love you
i sd, & she sd something
abt my children.

not even soap opera &
*cosmopolitan*
can take blame.
                        i know
they have long been witches
courtesans, succubi.
a foreign mouth.


## UNTITLED

two gloves
thin & blackish brown
grasping each other

what hands are absent?
what loves?

## LETTER TO KIRBY DOYLE

six years between greetings
six years of america
relentless america comic book world
issue after issue of super madmen in costume
on billboards in brains in our eyes flying

we cd compare
our journeys thru those years
make pain lists
madness itemizations
data indexes of inter-reality media
it wd be an unreadable poem
which we have both read
it read it in our faces, & our flesh
as we, still functioning, walk to each other's touch

the list of names of those we love who have fallen
is imprinted on our tongues
& need not be spoken

long years & hard times
hard times & much love
the past is present in our wounds
& in the healing magic
still surviving

## *UNTITLED*

the streets are filled with practiced gesture
dances concise & traditional
rhythmed prayers for protection

beyond, dimly seen, the edges
fall away.  these are paths
unmarked, which cannot be denied.
these depths of shifting patterns
offer no safety
to those who
do not dance in the uncharted shadows

here, it is a risk
to reach for a nother's hand

clumsy, tone-deaf, rejected
the dwellers in darkness know
they cd go back, be part of
the festive centers.  few do

the limits
of prescribed movements
cannot tempt the discoverers
of new ecstasies
new terrors
new faces for their children
to wear in the masks of darkness


## UNTITLED


o lady of verse, Lady of song, great & unbelievably exquisity Goddess
                                        of all living
as you are the ocean
as you are the earth
as you are the cunt of my beloved, filling my mouth & my soul
as you permeate everything with love & terror
as you have given me the third eye with which to see you & put me thru
            sufficient pain to be aware of you

i keep trying to say
thank you
some way, o my Lady, who must be
laughing, how many times
i must make you laugh

as if it isnt likely i'm not even
there, in yr
calculations, a tube to be flowed thru

that i shd be that tube
that you shd flow
                let it continue
                let the Goddess mouth continue to use my tongue hands
                        cock eyes feelings life

o Lady
if there are to be no more poems or paintings
if you were to disappear from my room, my world, my life
let it be that still
        when walking up & down
let it be that
        when moving thru the world
i can look up at yr face in sky & pay you
                homage
there cd never be a proper
homage

        o my Lady o my Lady o my Lady

  o Lady, Lady, come to visit my
humble house &
  humble it.  there are no
children there, there is no
woman
there.  it awaits You, Yr presence.  four walls & a narrow couch
a painting table & paints
a typewriter & paper & poems & the
accoutrements of
being

(at Yr will

      a poet.


        how to say thanks to the Muse!
Lady, Yr magnitude is undreamable, even by poets who
dream nothing but
You, Yr presence


  o Lady
  take touch tenderly throw me in the abyss of despair
  where the shining words sing & shimmer in the darkness of
                                   anguish


walking down the beach
walking down the ocean front walk
walking in & out of my heart
walking in the soul
walking in the world
walking the beautiful wet cunt of love
walking in the suns brite face
walking in the canals & their dirty water


    praises to Thee for my blindness, that i dont see what's coming
    praises to Thee for my worthlessness, that i know nothing &
                      seek to know
    praises to Thee for my love, that there are those who love me
                beyond all reason, loving that which You
                have inexplicably placed within my eyes
    praises to Thee for the light
    praises to Thee for the pain
    praises to Thee for the woman you have given to love me
    praises to Thee for Thy Self, as i see Thee ever the water silvering
                with moonface the holy explosions of the waves
    praises to Thee for the trees
    praises to Thee for my eyes, my eyes to see, to desire, to know
                                  Thee

for all these all the other gifts blessings lives bestowed upon me
that i know that i am unworthy, as any human must be unworthy
that You can still gift us with Yr presence
that i may know poems as they tear thru me on their way to the world


## THE DEATH OF ARTHUR

the king's death
        (witnessed by the last of
        the faithful

the last quest
        (triumphed by the water arm
        reaching

what can i do as they take him across the water?
what can i do as they lament his passing?


2. SONG TO BEDIVERE

lonely man
guilty man
at nite in the castle, remembering

remember first
the great deeds, yrs & theirs

remember next the maidens
of fair virtue

remember the death of the king
the last to go

o lonely man
o guilty man

313

bearer of lies to the dying king
false betrayer of the dying king
final companion of the dying king


3.

now they bring the boat
across the waters
now the dark singing comes
across the waters
now the dead virgins come
across the waters

finishing centuries of waiting in a single act
the maidens come
achieving their true meaning after centuries of waiting
the maidens come
bringing peace & haven to the patient king after centuries
                                        of waiting
the maidens come

o see the black flame
that plays across their eyes
o see the black tongues
that flicker in their mouths
o taste the black milk
that flows from their black breasts
o hear the black chants
that lament from their lips
o touch the black skin
that covers tite their black bones
o smell the black perfume
mingled music from their black boat
dance, king dance!
sing, king, sing!
yes! yr joy flows!
yes! yr voice shouts!

now you return
now you are received
now you may rest


4.

he believes that he will pass into time
will he pass into time?
he has passed into time

he believes that his name will be sung
will his name be sung?
his name has been sung

he believes that his ways will die
will his ways die?
his ways have died

he believes that he will be loved by god
will he be loved by god?
he is loved by god


## AT THE MASQUERADE


1.

with love
(that versatile tool)
the betrayers fill their terror

hands impromptu crammed
with lethal deceptions

they move in imitation dance
the images of their gesture blur

their eyes, confuse
actual definition
deny the physical
thing itself, its
solidity inviting hands
to human put hands on it, itself
open, a demand, a grasping

what is at risk?  their game of control, as the
all green & grow were not
flung fragrant into winds
continual transformation!
new! unvisioned! unhuman! joyous! undeniable!

rigidly identified, they map & read maps, learn
            words, use gestures of anonymous distance
such gestures are not dance
they are exhausted by the total
futility of knowing
their inevitable
failure.  at their game.
their game of touch, to which
they offer hands
warped rigid with holding
all movement, structure, desire, known
limits specific of the
flesh / body / the secret
other / it is a reach
of absolutely certain


2.


despite their inventive costuming
they find no unyielding boundaries
unannounced some seemingly
long dead thing
flowers  /  explodes
it has fire
it has earth

it has air
it has water
it has all, all, a turbulence
forming terrors cling to shreds of mask
violating costume's shattered facade
desperate they call out ambiguous names
with which they attempt to cloak a fear
so enormous & flab, so vicious & tender

              as tho they
authored it
they watch rot/animal/dance flow
past the polish
of their fear wet
unblinked eyes


## A POEM AT THE BEACH, IN COMMEMORATION OF JUNE 25/26, 1956, FOR MY WIFE.


The old man, on this grey, clear day
      (its sharpness outlines his figure
              like gleaming)

leans on his stick.
They are both bent & twisted.
His hair seems, at this distance, to be thick, tho white,
& his body seems vigorous
& is very tan.
Yet he walks, & uses, as aid, a stick.
& his other arm thrust out
as balance, the way men walk, who use canes.

        Of course, it must be admitted,
the sand is very difficult to walk on.

Leans & walks on this sand towards the ocean.
The brightest thing about the day
is the blue of his trunks.

An old woman sd to me: "Every day he does this. You know,
some people, they get old,
they don't know what they say, what they do,
as they get older they get crazier."

The old man, on this grey, hard, day,
bends his body
vigorously
at the water's edge,
& walks into its wetness.


UNTITLED


Moving from bed to bed
              & hating hating

how there are images evolved
           to pin to the wall of self
              to throw knives

at them, & spit

                women?
                    who do this?

pinning to the emptiness of walls
         moving from man to man
              hating hating hating


318

# UNTITLED

Shelley Manne, wild & out of his mind
with the need to sound, the music & his rhythms,
with not a waste beat or tone, each rap & stroke
so sharp & clean as to blind the ear, on the
night of August 13, 1956, sd/

The city streets
of hard
like sharp things
punching the eyes as they are
walked
       & black
with dirt & blood

          seeming the
death of all human rhythms
horns & thorns
blasting all eyes eyes
until there are no earth spots
for feet to grasp
to communicate

         They have their rhythms
       They have their drums
     They have their song

Throbbing the head
with blood filled eyes

Expanding ecstasy wombed
in the soul

until it threatens to
explode the boned skull

they have their magic
& their Gods

Somehow breaking thru
the crusted earth

Somehow once again
filling the air with fresh

Somehow once again
    singing swinging singing

feet to earth,
man, there is a swing
in a life

are there rhythms to breathe?

while we lie on our beds
& howl

& enter the houses of terror
begging


SIGHT, EGO & DESIRE / A LAMENTATION


Aie!  Aie!  Aie!
        Eyes, I's, & eyes
the soul's own confusion, for
some eyes
are flecked & twisted
        aie! aie!  they move
in pain, & have no focus

there are
    clear eyes
        aie,

the clear I's
    that have good color,
        strong eyes

& pierced aie's
      forced &
        hardened

eyes, I's, & eyes
        aie!  aie!


## UNTITLED


Charley laughs
      like the whole world
of that, my skin,
whips itself to foam, & makes such
a tension as to cause
      paralysis

Charley's laughing
put pleasing
& Charleywild
is a love sound sounding
on my whole
           largest functionism

pinbibbling it
  with
     chortles of

funny
    ecstasy

*UNTITLED*

delicacy, in a form
whether actual

        or abstract
harshly line & triangled, of steel
        or the warm soft
        breasted flesh
moving quietly, domestically

    makes
a pleasant tenderness
to breathe


*UNTITLED*

Good for Goodman
& cats of his ilk!

   Yes
      (tho there was a
      terrible corruption there

       good for
the swingtime!  It swung
the best it cd

       They had something
round & cool
  & they pounded away
inside it
  till it was a hardened & sharped
& edged
     thing of flat sides &

bumps
            quite square
                        in total shape

But, they, somehow
from their own needs

made it roll
along
    almost like a ball


*UNTITLED*


a broken chunk of yellow luxuriously lemon lollipop moon
lolls laying lazing in a child's midnite darkest velvet
                        dream sky.
in the distant citys, tall & scared
painters are striping escape hatches into the air
& all the cubscout drum & bugle boy parading children
hack at their strangling knapsacks
thrust cubmasters into the ocean
leap long pipedreamed disintegrating sounds
thru the abstract marshmallow buildings
thru the sticky taffy air.

lollipopping bugle bopping ten toe topping water slipping
mouths of open candy hungry eyes.


VARIATION ON A LETTER TO JONATHAN WILLIAMS


Yr mention of Zukofsky
brings to mind

others,
poets little read.  Of his
I remember parts of "A" scattered in magazines,
a poem
in an old *Poetry Chicago* called
"Mantis"
& a few others.

That is not a life.  A life's
work.

     Others have left
        (with me
           even less
A man named
Herman Spector
in & around *Dynamo*  in its day

Sol Funaroff
     who chanted to gatherings
all that pain & sympathy

Harold Rosenberg
turned philosopher

     Arensberg, collector
of paintings

     is he dead?
are all these men dead?

     Of those alive, which one still
writes at the poem?

Yes, Zukofsky
is still swinging "A"
thru the world
     but the others /
a mystery.

What do they record,
I wonder, from wherever they are?
What do they record, of their lives
& visions of loneliness?
                    What do they say
of us?


ii

the word.
its value.  & weight.

Man, are we in, then, a dream
by inmates?
              think, man!  call
it into yr head, this picture,
the poet
        (by which I mean myself, or you, yrself, man,
standing hobbled to his wall
& striking out in his crippled fashion
at the world that he feels, at him, tearing

& these men!  all these men
standing as he stands, there, & they too,
striking striking

                    see us as standing
without them,
think it man!  Hobbled & halfblind
with them there!

                    & what of them?  I cannot even
                    begin to imagine the extent of their
                    aloneness

to put all that sound down
& never know the effect

& I remain obsessed
with bitter endings

*UNTITLED*

Fleshuglied
flabbyarmed woman
under a street lamp
gabbering & swallowing word noises
with sloppy tongued
indifference

                as an idiot attempts
to feed himself by pushing
his face into the bowl
& breathing

PRELUDE TO PERCUSSION

Swing, man, there
the two deepest tones of love
one against & tenderly
the other

                sound sound sound
thrumm bumma booomm
            che bawah!  Bop! adop!

Slammy all the eyes
       the two deepest tones
             (one under my feet
      the other
          in my ear)

Sound, Chico, sound Leonard,
        blow
             ho ho

blow! man!
      Swing there?
            He
                  swings
                        there

man!

## A SAYING POEM

My wife has given me an image.  Of tall, & stunted, trees,
healthy & sick, half dead & dying, twined & skinned one the
inside of the other so deep do they meet

growing themselves & their others into their world outside
a hothouse, of green & warmth, in which there resides a
sweet pale orchid, beckoning out, beckoning, but repulsing,
always

saying, O, poor dears, that you are so stunted the some into
the other, & in here so warm, so warm.

The image tells of a winter, & sun, a swinging & a dying, in
the seasons, in this garden, whiteness & growth, the death
all pain & horror

two trees twining & groping even higher
than the rest, winterkilling each other their deepest horrors,
but in the sun flowering in new strength.

My wife, her soul an enormous womb of wildness, into the
life blasting

has called this a marriage story.

This image, this story, the laying bare of souls & freedom,
that followed, have called me to the voice to do a saying
poem, to say

to say / there is a love.  Always there are those that doubt,
        but there is a love.

to say / there is a love

to say / there is a love

There are trees, & there is a dark hardness in them.
They have been thru the twisted shapes of the garden, now they
stand & breathe.  They breathe a little deeper, a little wider,
& the dark hardness strengthens.

As the sun shines, they flower, & when there is a death around
them,
& the death beats & beats at them, & hurts them, & the orchid
beckons, & there is a hurt, a terrible pain,

the dark hardness backs itself to itself/
they grow.

To say / There is a love.

There is a way, to do, to get to the heart of something. There
is in existence a body of techniques for experiencing, & per-
ceiving a reality.

There are things to do, to get into the meanings, of our
fears.

Usually, they involve the asking of questions.
Answers, possibilities of reactions, out of somewhere deep,
pounding & tearing, hurting & prodding to growth

open the road out of the garden of despair, out of the tangled
pipes & broken cement, the flashing wires, the piles of in-
different corpses, rotting, flowers growing out of them, rats
sliding & fucking in the crevices of the flesh,

to a place where there are growing things.

> Answers do this. If the questions are faced. & the wildness
> is opened, inside.

> This is a time, where we live now,
> filled of terror & things done to us, & others, filled of
> decay & stench.

> Fearscreamed in the night of history, it bleeds scum over the
> name of man.

> This is a time, where we now live,
> that takes its young, its own births, & slowly, with the ex-
> quisiteness of a practiced sadist, torments the shapes of their
> souls until their indescribable nightmares overwhelm reality,

> & places on them a responsibility to rigidity, a hatred of
> love. & fear.

In this time, devoted to destruction, & terror, devising its
theology from the agony of its people

there are not many questions asked.  To receive answers.

So, not many answers are received.

But we know, there are ways, to do, from different eyes, to
get into a reality.


## A NIGHT WHEN MY HATREDS WERE FORCED OUT INTO THE OPEN BY THE PRESSURES OF LOVE


                I fled screaming into my own wounded
past,
                 looking wildly over my shoulder, left &
right, each shift of the eyes occasion for a new terror,

              & met, along the way, dark hungry images
of myself.
            Some, their faces half swallowed by rot,
the waiting half with legs parted to receive its destroyer

            others with penises driven into their
eyes, who spoke only in half formed hoarsenesses

            all these faces faced to mine, these
stenches rotting in all our nostrils

            shouting my name & my pain, begging for
sympathy, or holding up torn hands in chains mutely whimpering
to be beaten

            shouting & moaning & grotesquely re-
enacting

my own deepest violences.

As I saw them,
one by one, fall to their knees before me,

I made animal noises
& tore my teeth thru soft things

jammed thumbs into my eyes,
to not see

closed in my lungs
to not breathe

pounded my head against
any deadly object
to not hear

& in this state
went swiftly to a dark
& lonely place

There was an arm around me

I moaned & shrieked & gibbered into deeps
of stasis

& pain was there

Embrace me  / it sd, I am a door. Break
thru.  & see.  Be cleansed.

I had forgotten how much it hurts
I had forgotten terror
I had forgotten loss

& enclosed me.

O God!  O God!

# THE OMINOUS THELONIOUS

monks around the cocoanuts
monking blues & down the black & white trees

wam de bam!
go slow
open that head man
& blow!

wild & wail
the inner voice
the nail/in the arm
the choice/on the sword
the child
singing in the dark

monk!  mark the chalk
of life
on yr eyes

obop sh'bam!
sh'bam bam!

# THELONIOUS MONK DISCOURSES ON LOVE

to give & not to give

love

mainline
a
wham

da bop!

Eyes!

& sing wild songs
1922
        get outa here
we're breaking thru!

gone
gone

come back
come back

 Eyes!
    man!
       eyes!
          is!
            the!
              thing!


UNTITLED


There is a cat
sitting on a pile of manuscripts.
She chaoses neatnesses.

        (Can it be that I hear the verse,
          under her, on the paper that she is on
        also

                its structure never
                at any time
                too stable

                        shattering?)

As she extends her leg
in the classic stance, & grips it
with two paws,
brushes her tongue over it, purring,
my eyes hold upon the meat of her thigh,
its thickness,
& I image shredding it,
tearing it from the bone with my teeth.
I can almost taste
the warmth.

        In my wildness
I even find
        the texture of fur
in my mouth

        quite pleasant.


## UNTITLED


Do parents know, what they do, when they pass to their children

the fear of death?

Is it a conscious part of that struggle to break the new growth,

push it out of the sun, spread the aged foliage over its head to rob it of light,

absorb water intended for its roots, block all areas of expansion

which is so much a part of all growing & dying?

Or is it simply that
they can themselves no longer live
the guilt
& must unload onto
their children, a vomiting, a
sickness
they spread?

It is, of course (one is amazed to discover), simply another
one of their lies.

It is a lie important in the fabric of
lies they weave their love thru,
weaving & crossing,
designing patterns of evil
in the cloth of other souls.

Now that it is seen to be a lie, I wonder that I ever be-
lieved it.


SOI DISANT SALON
*for Lachlan Mac Donald*


Behind my transparent wall

    (but which of us is the
    patient, & which
    the doctor)

I watch people take words
into their hands
& throw them flatly on the floor
somewhere in the vicinity of the person
addressed

A word, hits the floor
with a rather, quiet
thud

It is difficult to try
to point out to them what they are doing.
They do not want to
hear

I cannot speak to them
to say /
                    take the thrusting force
into yr hands, the word
to be gripped stroked, caressed
kissed
& finally
        all other areas thoroly explored
                        received

They think they are the doctor
& I am insane
I think I am the doctor
& I am insane
& they too

I have the feeling that someone has gathered these poets
together,
set into motion forces which drive them to grope
for language

            &, thru a one way mirror
            hands thrust deep into the pockets of his
            starched white coat

                    this someone sits behind
                    his transparent wall
                    he knows which is the doctor
                    & which is the patient

is laughing
at the whole
spectacle


## UNTITLED


we come on quiet
man
moving down the street

       loaded!  loaded with misery!

like we don't know each other
man
as we pass & touch

       loaded!  loaded with misery!

we shuck each other about love
man
& tell terrible lies

by not looking at the eyes
man
we invite disaster

       loaded! loaded with misery!

## UNTITLED

ASKED ABOUT PAIN I SD/
EMBRACE IT.  IT CLEANSES / LIKE A KNIFE CUTTING CUTTING AWAY DEAD
TISSUE.  IT OPENS YOU UP.  YOU CAN SEE.

ASKED TO CONSIDER SUFFERING I SD/
IT SEEMS SOMEHOW SUPERFICIAL IN RELATION TO PAIN

PAIN IS A DOOR.  A GATE / I SD /
ONE OF THE DOORS MOST AVAILABLE.  THRU THE PAIN WE CAUSE OUR
SELVES & OUR LOVE WE CAN EXPLODE THRU UNHEALTHY FORCES/RIDE
THEM OUT/ LIVE THEM

BREAK THRU &   SEE.   ARE CLEANSED.

I FORGOT HOW MUCH IT HURTS.
I FORGOT ABOUT TERROR.
I FORGOT ABOUT LOSS.


## SPRING LAMENT

this is the year
Persephone has forgotten
                (or, perhaps, just didnt
                want to make it

it was spoken of
matted beards rose & fell excitedly, once
speaking of it
the bleakness of it

                this now dull landscape speaks well
                of their sight


338

here the dawn is grey
the ground is hard

Pluto has at last gotten his way


*UNTITLED*


What is it?  over the man's head,

covering some space.

It doesn't keep off the atom bombs

or help him fly.

Can he wrap himself up in it at night

while he sleeps,

or dreams?

Sometimes at the beach

    they have bright stripes


People sell hot dogs

    under them


When the wind blows, the rain

comes in

      anyway.

## UNTITLED

in the movies

it's always so cool

    against the wall

bang!

    (snuck up

        pushed the thing

            on me

bang!
don't I even get

a last

    cigarette?

bang!

# ON SINAI

*An Egyptian woman*
*a child disguised*
*a river*
*To lovers of the Word*
*These are the Word*
                    (Gr. Anthol. I; 59)

## I

I don't want to go back there.

I don't want to go back there

where they are waiting.  All the years the years

& I have always known.  I don't want to go back

there!

      I remember

when as a child I took the hot coal,

to save myself for this.  For this!

Why, when I rose to say 'O my People'

didn't I stammer so badly that they might laugh

at me,

      & throw sand & dust into my flushed face

make me the clown instead of

the leader.

I've always known.

Look at them, anxiously waiting

the sun

reflecting off their few poor weapons

their loins lusting after the land.

Even now

some are after their women.

& the children watching, laughing.

       I don't

want to go back down there

with this Law.

What do they know of the meaning

of a covenant?

They've always followed me

not knowing what a cruel thing

a God is.

       I should have taken the gold,

then, when I was a child, & ended it.

I knew it then.

       A prophet's eyes behind my eyes

wouldn't let me.  Now I'm old, & hold in my hand

this tablet.

What do they want

of me?  I could

destroy these now.


(there is a sound of thunder)


No, don't shout at me.  I

know you are there.  Once before

I had a chance to destroy you

by letting your people go into the slime

of decadence & slavery,

& the angel,

the damned angel

talked against it until my poor child's mind

knew nothing but glory.  So you won.

But now I am old, & I'm not afraid.

I remember

how it was when I was young

& lived in the palace of the king.

His daughter loved me,

saved me from the river.

I remember, I remember,

Her breasts were nice

                         the nipples

red.

She fed & wrapped me,

told me I was a prince.

                    What

years

the first years are

when they are as mine were.

All those down there then

worked or watched their fathers work

building with strawless brick

for the pleasure of the king

& me.


& then the choice!  The gold or coal,

& the angel with his voice

sweeter even than the princess' loins,

whispering to me of the future,

of the people out of bondage, into

their land.

He flashed a picture into my mind,

& it took me with it to this place.

I saw then

        (as I could see now were I standing

         away from

         myself on this high rock

the Godword in my hand

the people

below, waiting

in the sun.


It took me

& I went with it.  & here

I am now.

        I don't want to go

back there!

        But I went with it

because I saw

myself as creator of a People

& of a God.  I chose it,

moulded them, brought them to this place

where they now wait.

I did it myself.

I brought myself here.

I made them mine.

I must give them

their Law, their tormentor.

I saw it happening, then, my hand clutched

at the gold,

saw it happen now

    (more clearly, even than now

        an angel's eyes are clear, clear eyes

I cannot deny what has already

occurred.

        I will return to them.

Back, down there.

## II

From the mountain, rock fell,

followed by the blazing tongue

(no longer stammering):

> "Is this your

> worship?  Self-Interest

> betrays you, that dance

buys

nothing."  Crumbling law

between his teeth, he turned his back.


> Murder!  Murder!

Was it a stone, or a knife?  Perhaps

a heavy jewel, one of the animal's

false eyes, a ruby

smashing the base of the brain,

bringing the unexpected reprieve

from exile.

III

Dancing

still dancing

they travelled into the land

from which history split off

in many tides.

The wind

of their songs moved dust on

the desert, pushing fragments

this way, & that.

      "What are years in exile,

      O my land?

      What are tears of exile

      on my hand?

      Joyous are years in exile

      O my Lord.

      Strong are tears from exile

      on my sword."

How many years,

slowly traveling, one by one,

did it take to piece together

the fragments?


At a different mountain

the volcano spoke,

& the same-named priest,

ignorant of previous crime,

reproclaimed the accusation:

"Is this

your worship?"


At the sound of this

the people prostrated themselves,

packed their few belongings

& moved under sterner discipline,

leaving behind all gold,

all rubies,  daggers, lutes,  concubines,

taking only

the self-slashing ritual,

the prayer shawls, the book,

& the memory of white teeth

gnashing the Law to foam & blood & dust.


## MR. FERDINAND JELLY ROLL MORTON

This man put many faces on himself.
He filled his mouth with hard sharp lies
that gleamed their traces thru his song.

He built his life's monuments
with few tools
& no guides to the building of them,
making them up out of his great wild head
as he went along,
never looking backward as he fled,
building new beginnings, stuffing them in his face
to be chewed
& by his strong ten hands spewed into the ear.

With his hundred hands
he shaped many figures,
labelling this one, singing that one,
until the music & the many men
became so commingled & denied

that it was, in the end,
the piano itself they carried off,
ten thousand of its hands
screaming & playing on its own head its own songs.

*UNTITLED*
*a poet, that is to say a prophet, a voice a creator*
—Henry Miller


a voice

the voice

the sound


      & music

        is a sound


when the poet

falls

        in the forest

alone

is a sound

        (actually?

made?

music

music

is a sound

# LETTER TO MY YOUNGER BROTHER

*(upon receiving from him a brush drawing of two boys on
halloween, one masked, the other sheeted, as a ghost)*

the world's glee
to dress itself in games
from underneath the shirt
to draw the knife

to see our own unseen
face
we look at faces

hands
hands
it's as tho there werent
any

we see
laughing mouth
bright eyes
laugh at
noses

knives & poems
move in & out of hands
while we dream a face
for our empty skulls

these kids swing along
but
what hands are hidden clumsily
in their masks?

*UNTITLED**

went down there, o
singer, went down there, o
luteman

after that girl. to where
they didnt dig song or
singing

showed you knew who to
believe.  climbing down those walls. hugging
yr horn

after, after the stoning, & that whole scene,
to float yr head down the ocean
spouting trade secrets

to the lesbians /

that was a cool touch


—*to orpheus*

---

* This poem is a variant of "To Orpheus," pp. 195-6 in this edition.

there are utter fascinations
in the problems of power

take Moses / what he did

"behead the
brat
    grabbed the crown, he
seeks his place"
                  now to a child a problem, a choice
                  pushed by the angel
                  within his sight were all the endings

utter fascinations, for
who will not believe his first consideration
was the gold
               he was, in spite of, what happened, later, human
               & who cd resist the escape, the freedom
               after seeing merely that first ending
at the foot of the mountain /
                       to have done all that only
to be greeted by the golden animal
& on top of that
           (murdered

"no, man, it is just a child's
prank, the briteness shines his hand
to it"

          (for look / he had it within his mind
          to cloak the motives
          & whispered to his Lord
          of all the horrible endings
          from that time on
          hoping to get permission)

      & cd he not see into our own world?
      wdnt that be enough to convince him?
      who can argue with it?


2.

but history
(accepting it makes a certain basis
has it differently

      "i say, put him to a test
      a coal & a coin, both of brite aspects
      which he chooses decides / the flaming beauty
      of the power symbol"

      & the other one sd: "behead the brat
      or y'll regret it"

the king of course decided to be kingly
& chose the test
& the child chose

      the problem is /
               why?

history has it /
      that the angel pushed his hand after he had
made his choice &, the murder of a God in his hand, had
reached
for the gold, to end it, there

      the angel? pushed? the prophet
      of prophets
      tampered with by an angel?

      clearly false
simply what
a historian might want the people
to believe

3.

there are certain possibilities

he cd have become involved
with his image in history
& taken himself
to arms

    or cd he have been attracted
by a genuine
religious experience?
           he might have known other things
unrecorded

      utter fascinations sing
in the problems of power


## AN UNSCIENTIFIC POSTULATION[*]
*i do not believe that god plays dice with the universe*
—Albert Einstein

1.

the sea the source, the womb
life crept from.  rivers
feed it / their known
function.

the body's river, blood, what
is its ending, its
origin?  known
as life, as death, its ultimate

---

[*] This poem includes some lines that also appear in an untitled poem beginning "That which is man," pp. 100-102 in this edition.

mechanisms remain mysteries.  red, it
is the body's food.  that
is its sum.  man
can identify it, its surface.
put the knife to any throat / to the eye
the flowing is the same.


2.


as time is counted blood
of jews was known
poison.  this history.  a convenience.
hides the earth red
saturated.  known red, its course
traceable.  maps
have been drawn, experiments
made.  even identities fatally
unmixable are known.

as time
is, as history is.


3.


only jews have concern with this, & those
whose function
is be their murderers.

as time
is counted, by the counters
of time.

the river within the flesh / what
hides there?  a jew knows
he is a jew / a fact also known
to his murderers?  known
in the unknown ocean, the encompassing
river? the nourisher, the destroyer?
the blood?


TIGER CAT
TIGER CAT
YOU DONT KNOW WHAT Y'RE LOOKING AT.


teeth bare
eyes flare
a savage joy
not to destroy

the tiger cat girl pounced
(her hair was a lightning storm)
(glimpsed thru the crook of an arm

but she was not cautious, or discreet
(altho my shoulder bears her teeth)
i saw her flash from below like a knife.
i waited to feel  .   to bring me to life
cut away all decay, make
real.

tiger cat woman, sharp toothed, brite eyed
scarred belly. soft movements. claws. longest rides.
here, here is my shoulder, my arm.
whatever part you want. to devour. to keep warm.

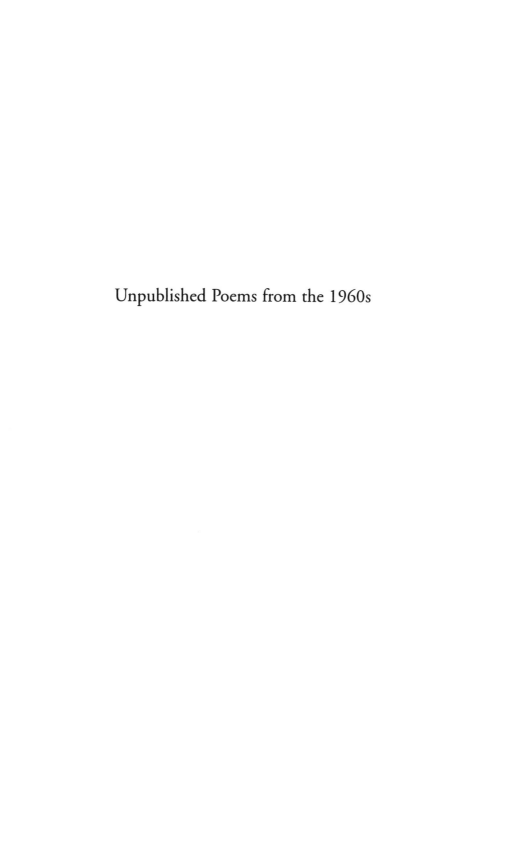

Unpublished Poems from the 1960s

Lady, my soul, naked, shivering
cold in its fear & love, trying to wrap its no arms around
                    itself for a little
warmth
black soul of
human destruction, black soul of
human pain, my pain, mine, my pain, yr gift
black with hate & love
black with children & looted graves
black with being the knife sliced sacrifice
to yr limitless power
black my black soul is
yrs, & this
notebook, as naked & exposed
is yrs.

come to me lover, mother, muse
if yr desires demand my
soul of black &
fear, my tongue hammered to pulp
my eyes that see only
what you reveal to them

come to me, these naked pages
fill them with my screams & prayers
fill them with You, the butterfly wing of my dreams.

# NEW YEAR POEM IN LATE FEBRUARY

*man is to man a beast: a fawning dog, a roaring lion, a*
*thieving fox, a robbing wolf, a treacherous jackal, & a*
*rapacious vulture.*

—Kenneth Patchen

we walked the bridges in a time
of dead tongues. this winter.
cold moon on the sky. ice eyes
staring into the fog. slow.

the whole pack with ice on their faces, clogging their ears
thick, like
a glass helmet
from shouting into the dirty snow
under the dark.

tired moon. tire dances.
cold times, ice on bridges.
nothing growing. nothing.

it's a good thing
spring
comes

(really does
arrive

air
color
rain
rivers breaking, moving

earth brightens.

She walks.

voices of others can be
distinguished.  still distant
but.
       coming closer.


## INVOCATION
### for John Thomas


in winter's dungeon mouth & mumbling tongue
forsaken by the ice of winter prayer
half-scream, not frozen in the solid air
with plea & praise of birth ice-clogged, unsung.
my sluggish eye follows the gulls at wing.
they dance their screeching laughter at my feat,
my groping fingers break & disappear,
my eyes are coffins, hidden from the sun.

this fallow field I pray you will re-seed.
these frozen eyes I pray you burn with flowers
as yr floods up surge life over the sand
do not bypass the parched mouth of my need
Release my throat from winter's dazzled towers:
O Lady, plant your kiss up on my head


## UNTITLED


Lady, in yr blackest dress you swoop into our eyes
twist love into a noose, & gaily
dangle poets over pits
of yr laughter

you know you have taught us well how to hurt
how to feel the chill & terror
as yr hands grow claws, as yr eyes are masked,
    as yr breasts become daggers

in the lite of the full moon of yr face
all hidden corners of our souls
are illumined like a vision of yr kiss
hot, &
glowing, destructive, blinding, hypnotic, &
tender


*UNTITLED*


we carry our crises within our heads
our arms drip them
our fingers tear at
them

move thru destruction
towards peace?
so what?
in the gut the huge cities of murderers
of beggars
of starving people

animal, animal, yr teeth
drip blood. i know it is warm
& red. what
made me think
i wd not meet you here?

since birth i am
an exile.  not counting
the roads.  traveled or
avoided.

in moments of rare
hope i have
even set markers on
the trail.
as tho others
wd follow.

running & hiding away
& towards
not knowing
either

flight.  boned
terror in my eyes.
in my rush breathing dust
& corpses.  i dont
speak the tongue
dont know the customs
yet i
am, tho
survival is surely
impossible in such
circumstances.

always, always, the push
ing out, never the
ingather, the
coming home.

# UNTITLED

closed, flowers seem modest, humble
within their petalled refuge
vibrate luminescent color revelations

flowing, moving, energies run like rivers towards
the great deeps, the source, the cycle of reawakening

leaping in, swept up, i am carried along
not moved by the currents, becoming one with movement
into it, part of it, swift, expanding, overflowing
growing, laughing, swirling in the sunlite, glittering

i am the dance the dancer moves thru
i am the sound of the voice chanting poems
over falls, thru gorges, the music of earth in my flesh
i am the joy in the laughter of birds

"we cross & we do not cross
the same rivers
we are & we are not"
                        sd heraklitus

moving over the stone & song
the rise & fall of the waters' breathing
shapes my visions

& all direction & intention
folds over on itself
enclosed in the bud's balanced tenderness

*UNTITLED*

see my dead eye
not twinkle dead eye
pot poet eyes dead my dead
eyes i have to
carry in my head
dead


*UNTITLED*

venice is
venice used to be
i mean
it hardly seems the thing
poems talk paintings

except the thing learned
the thing quite safely
horrifying

*UNTITLED*

the poem is
  the act.  the act is
  gesture, is
        (so obviously
  love

  love is no
  words, but it is
  to be
  human brings fears


*UNTITLED*

wrapped in time's
harsh web, thrust
into its false & forward
movement
i am suddenly
able to count.  check.
keep track of my
own disintegration

unable to pretend, i move in the now.  once
time's shreds of death
touch the bone
there is no forgetting it

matter (my very
flesh) is never
destroyed, i'm told.  is trans
muted.  muted as tongueless
giraffe, tree, or
grass blade whitman

sang.  using whitman's undumb
tongue.  i speak says
beckett because
i must.  because i
must.  & adds / but i do not
listen.  dumb as
any growth, growing thing
because i must, because
i must, i do / facing the ultimate
dead but not destroyed
me.  dumbtongued.


## UNTITLED


MAN MAKES
A LARGE IMAGE OF
MAN.
        FLESH.  BONE
STRUCTURING THE
WHOLE THING A
BONE BALANCE

HAS IN IT INTERPLAY
OF SUCH COMPLEXITY
STRUCTURES, NETWORKS.  THE
LIVING CELL
MAINTAINS ITSELF.  MAINTAINS
ME, AS I
AM FLESH.  AM
MAN.

MAN TURNS ON HIS OWN
WEARS DEATH IN HIS MOUTH
IS INVENTIVE IN
MAN-TORTURE.  HIS HISTORY
RESEMBLES HIS
FACE:          DISINTEGRATING.

BUT GIVE TO
ANY CREATURE THE OPPOSING
THUMB.  IT WILL FIND
ITS TOOL. WILL FIND ITS POWER, ITS DEATH, ITS
TERROR IN ITS NEW HANDS.


## UNTITLED


no words
again
an ode to
silence
which blankets
babble & makes
lies
more difficult
to form


## UNTITLED


So take your time to task
not humanity
          with its while away
societies of nothing on their hands.
My tune is tasky keen

and
droll with do enough that never is.

Unlikely this that has me off again
in tear and hate to go
                          away from liked
him even if he was
or acted like.

To positively love and long to,
can halve your soul same
intwo starfish reproductiveness
that blends the hateful left behind
with stronger than before.
                          So onto-
into this dream of waking up from.

Belabor like in asking if you will,
but I must be off again in waiting.

Carefree fight for food and fucking fine
girls who wander in the night
                          of manlessness;
unmindful
           when there was
one, 'cause who ever saw one before he came
and went,
           and afterall
who had the gall to send him
                          he has his nerve
at that.
Beseeching fruit from
                  rootless vines
grape gropingly.

One flirt farting fling at
say goodby
                  'till tears rend me depart
abruptly
           (did you see—he was crying).

He ought to be ashamed at what
he sees instead of.
                    After all,
who does he think he is
and all of that.

Brown eyes of conscious lip
                    like loving
leave him be with all his self contained,
in worthyness that reeks
                    of rotten spuds

—surplus for over seas
                    too late for starving

Clinker built arm pit strong
enough for seas of qualmness
rude at dawning,
                    far from here or
there—. what have you when it drys,
                    afterall one has to
be careful about stuff like that
only begotten son-of-abitch,
                    and who so ever quenches
the fire is a chickenshit.

Flog the air with your bookless
flanders smile
that wanders face to face
                    in coughing.
But let in the light and you'll
wipe out your little mushroom patch of dankness
lily wet yearning to be picked
                    and
                         plopped
                              into
                                   the

soupy keen, spanked by the wooden spoon
of lippy sip tasting slurp seasoning

too damned hot to cope with
                              so serve it up.
Whores and sailors don't care.

Of poems and painting balderdash
be careful lest they rip out your appendix
and tie your colon in a knot of
                              candid frolic
cutting up.

Keenly cautious count your whims and
ask for change—
                    it doesn't hurt to
                                        ask.
there is none.


*UNTITLED*


the sun is being devoured. lite of life. the moon is
eating my blood.

they are partners.  sun & moon, to get back into them my
body's heat. while the sky eye has a center of black circle
instead of flame.  a deep cavern of black in which to fall.
the sun & the moon are silently fleeing to the outer edges.

gone.   gone.  while i am hypnotised by the infinite pupil
that hangs in place of the burning.  of the lite.

                                        now i
stand shivered & chilled.  my blood green ice grows in my
stomach.  not the sun, the moon has betrayed me. as lovers
cry.  to the bone.

## UNTITLED

the natural history of the body is known.  hidden within its
own bones are the texts of its origins.  there glitter the
jewels of time.  gold explosions of lite.  deep & blooded.

it flows, the body.  is a river that carrys the seed from
the mountains.  is its own seed & delta.  growing, it is a
vine that strangles.  there are no limits to it.  flexible
& timeless, it washes away the edges.
not to be grown, it discovers itself.  reaches & opens,
hungry.  a mouth or hand.  it gestures, a tree.  it diminishes
lite, cuts bone into prismed fragments, twitches, a bird.

the body is a body of murder, a dance.  it reads its own song.
it has no face.  a woman, a man.  a grave & a voice.

the mystery of the single eye.


## UNTITLED

it is ancient sin
to attempt restructuring the universal
balance
            forgetting one's
place within human skin
                        gods dont feed
the green things carbon
do not take clarity & breath from the leaves & the earth
gods want this exchange facilitated
have man & other mammals
for this task
            if man resigns
in order to be better at godhood
those gods he knows, has known

374

wd be better than he even can conceive
wd be the best god for this possible world

cd i do as poorly
as has been done?  this reasonable
(let's look to what evil dance?)
question cuts urgently thru the smoke
& the thousand tiny explosions of flames devouring wood
overtones of richer texture
the boiling blood erupts the whole flesh
opens earth like a chaos of blackened flowers
blooming directly to ashes
which quickly cool & are grey, grey
dust mounds the wind spreads quickly into the hungry soil


## UNTITLED


my lady, my lady, what you demand
is surely beyond the reach of my hand.
my lady, my lady, to give form to love
is a gift that few poets ever receive.
my lady, my lady, who better than you knows
the poet is a splinter on the wave, who knows not where he goes.
my lady, my lady, yr indulgence i pray
that my failure to be what you want me to be will not offend you this day.


we are thrust into a formless world.  we inherit
chaos.  as children we hide in it, in the huge empty lots
filled with a long tough fibrous growth we called
horseweed.
pulled out by the root it was a spear, broken into short lengths
it was
            (we pretended it was, we actually smoked
                        it
                    smokable.

there were no boundaries to our world, then.
we dug caves with several rooms, masturbated, shot bb guns at each
others' eyes
set fire to whole areas of harsh weed
just find a pattern to
bump against, a form to
fit into.

we bleed, fuck, twist, grow, alone/
o man, you have masks
masked is yr face masked is yr soul masked is yr cock
masked is yr wife masked is yr religion, masked are yr children
faces behind the masks become the masks there are no faces
the emptiness is terrifying.
but masks are not forms.  what are
the rituals demanded by love?

only the bird wing against the cheek
gives a clue.  when i touch you, touch yr face, then i feel
the warmth.  real life.  when yr soft warm skin, so smooth & gentle
touches mine.  sucking yr sweet cunt flowerlike opening under my mouth
filling my mouth & my soul
then i know abt the true forms.
lady, o my lady, i hope pray
this might be the day
i get say all that i wanted
& meant to say

UNTITLED

into the river, it is a road. lifts & carrys. o its black
waters as they move, move,  move their dark selves. move
into the earth. the breath black. deep in.

where all is black, there is no sky. yet the trees thrust
up, tall. where there is no sky, all is hidden.  bracelets

of root on the earth's many wrists.  fat root, thick, twisting,
swallowed by the soil. to keep the trees earthed. they
are not permitted to follow their upward leap. to flight.

slow is the dance of the acolytes of stone.  within the temple
of the interior, pouring lite into the cup of the trees' mouths,
charms & birds weaving. mesh of dancing.

shifting, shifting, closing in.  in.  quieter & close.  flight,
the river, the song, the skyless wing.  all the dogs lie
still.  the trees are touching.

o the river that brothers the shift of the clouds, the
voyage itself asleep in its rocks & foam.  what a cold
womb!  born in the dark, giving forth in the dark. branch
to branch.  tree to tree.


## UNTITLED


sitting in the quiet breeze of morning
watching the copper-green & orchid metallic reflections off
                          the pigeons' feathered necks
round head, deep love throat junky pinpoint eyes
dancing the fluttering breadcrumb ritual
mirrored in the bluegrey ocean
sandpipers & gulls waiting their turns
at the edge of the magic circle
whisper of wind, warm in my ear
frankie & i, muse drunk in the soft air
venice morning, oceanfront walk
people of venice, smiling, sunned, enchanted
venice magic dazzling eyes with world, with city
with street & ocean, &
bird crys of deep tender softness

# THEME FROM "THE CHEATERS"

When we become sexual prey to one another,

    devouring flesh in lonesome night

When the hightide of warm bath

    bathes lust unrelinquished

When towering phalli overcome you in dreams

    of terror, spurting steam

And the maw of the cunt open, festering

    obscene

When the wild cry of the animal cries out

    exhausted ecstatic pain

When sex is reduced to the rubble of dry

    come and torn sore flesh

When the room reverberates with the loud

    bells of passion, dresses ripped the

    sheets also, and blood drying on face

    and hands

    Then God's sweet face smiles down.

    My children, he says, my children.

once i believed
no, i knew
the poem
a poem
the perfect poem
Her sound made flesh, made words
with perfect accuracy
cd transform
make man the angel he is within himself

make a world where
all speech was poem, all gesture, dance, all longing
singing, each movement of man's desire
that which he so desperately forms
within his dreams, memories of what
was, what can be

then i was thrust into
worlds inhabited by humans indescribable
altho i had known of them
i cd not believe when i saw them
what man cd be so . . so . . what i now know
man can be
can the poem touch
these?  cN THESE SO BEASTLY & undesiring
be
    transformed?

              i doubted, & the doubting
crippled me, cripples me

                   O lady, bring me back
to my faith in yr power

o Lady, do not abandon me to these
with their dollars in their pockets
with their hatred in their cocks
with their titless women, their wombless world of
no love, no fucking, no birth, no opening out


O Lady, do not abandon me to my own guilts & needs
only to be yrs.




*UNTITLED*


in the midst of life
there is
language

like a hairball
in the throat
or blood
clogging the needle




*UNTITLED*


1.

didnt they say
to get good poems
cut newspapers into words
& collage?
        tristan tzara.
that
takes care of meaning.

maybe in france you can, *gots you guts?*
throw it in the street
anyway no word or poem
ever destroyed.

tzara reminds me
art & literature are my enemies.  the precise
core.

have no real interest
in their streets
their milieu
                or in the ones who read it
solemnly

at least recognise with me its total
unimportance.  truly, only i care
whether this gets written

the act of the poem
when she makes you flower.  at
the root.


2.


the duck king sd/ "where we were
hardly mattered.  the pond
was ice.  we
had to come down.
it was very cold.  we huddled.
a man tried to kill us.
there arent many nice men."


3.


all it
really means cut up a
newspaper column.  or head

381

line.  or dr. crane.  so
funny all of them
so badly written
make magic with that
material
& poetry *is*
real!

there arent many nice
men.  the duck king told me
of their migrations
                    lucky
there are still
ways out & one can
cut newspaper anywhere.


## UNTITLED


a specific reality
can unfold like a new flower
from being held within itself
to an open thing, complete
thing

          (a completion, a circle
from desire to desire
fulfilments & certain
dissatisfactions

## UNTITLED

the birds.  on the beach
like clusters of dirty flowers.
huddled.  digestive.  the triumphant screech
stilled.  as tho it is willed the whole world be peaceful
      at this hour.

the sea.  silent.  no love
possible greater than its indifference.
it does not love, it does not reject, it does not strive.
greater than love its fertility, its omnipotence.

the people.  the sand, cooling
beginning to cool.  Venice at my back, facing the sunset.
gently relaxing the tender eyes of feeling
immersed in the rhythm of rest
watching the gulls.  they huddle.  they digest.

## UNTITLED

poets talk of magic in ritual, of magic in the word.  yet
the birds do not gather to listen to our chants.

"you all are poets, i myself am on the side of death"
sd rimbaud.  knowing it cdnt be done, he stopped trying.

we have a language we cannot touch.  cannot feel the
shape.  black words, yr streams contain man's poison.
yes! i also am a man.  only a bird can embrace a bird.
& yet we maintain the color of the flower exists only in our
eye & mind.

it is not so much man makes me vomit, but how he tries
to make his language real, lies to make his language
real.


## UNTITLED


man is stone on my tongue. i taste. even i must be immune
to love, or i will strangle.

no tooth, no claw, no wing. even wind can slice our soft flesh.
make bells of the bone. still we sing demented & lustful. my
blood moves thru my body. i am surprised it is such dark red.
no one knows how to call it.

this is the center of chaos, the eye. we breed shifting &
narrow.

stone in my mouth, bitter. bitter kisses, mocking & old. we
live today by a new deviousness.

i love the word like a bird, but it betrays. clogs my mouth
with stone. its taste & weight determine how i bleed.


## A SONNET OF SEPARATION FOR SUZAN / THE OATH


by holy wedlock locked, looked, locked, looking, leaking

by "true stories" magazine, mauled, marked, murdered, mad

by ten years filled with moons & children, moonchild glad

by each others' terror at what was sought, searched, seeking by every dead word strangled just before speaking

by the long hotel of remembering, dimlighted, aliceinwonderland faced.

                                  long overcoat clad

by all the gemlike diseased structures mangled, moved, destroyed

by the corpses in the corridor, retched, ripped, rotted, reeking


by all this, & more, & then more, & still more

by every breath breathed, by the bitter core

as tho my hand were monstrous huge & slammed

upon the gibberished bible of the damned,

as tho i heard my voice in loud, harsh tones

saying: 'i swear. we sucked the marrow from the bones.'


                    O PARA
                         / O DOX
                            —*a political poem*


                that day, so long awaited, when
                the walls crumble, & the light
                (supposedly) shines into
                        & all the rats
                            shrivel up into dust
                          & die

              is almost upon us.
                    O

      para/
   dox
        (we inside
wow!  the bricks
          praising them
but they're hitting us
on the head)
            this house is coredead

all the boys
(you can see it)
in a little circle around a table
   with a candle on it & a couple
of books
    planning this
  para/
 dox
    (they didnt know

they put into a small container
some powder
some glass
some gasoline
           (need i say
BOOM!)


2.

take the vision, take the fact.
the fact, the vision.
vact. fision.
      fission.

(boom!)

everybody (i remember it) was supposed
to be outside, marching up & down
everybody's arms around everybody else
&c.

out of the open doors of the factories
streams of men were thought of
their machines still turning on the power of

(if i remember it
                    (love
everything
clean, like rain
on it.  men
breaking out
of all shells
of terror
that hold them.

no more walls.
fields growing.
love alive.

                    o

          para
                    o
          dox

the vision.  the fission.
                            (need i say


3.


into all the darkest rooms the future slinks
its face dissolved in acrid smoke.
the walls are coming down
                            o down

     that circle
& their bottle/
               that bottle/
                            those
books/
          wow! the bricks.  can we praise them?

(they're hitting us/

                       need i say

boom)


### UNTITLED


how take
the tongue
to say
love

       (the thing is big, & stands
       as we stood, there, on the rock
       overlooking the water smashing
       leaving soft froth

       animals cower in the corners of my eyes
       leaping out & claws flying
       into air

into air, the nite
as She swings Her white ritual
thru the sky
expand
explode the hard rise & fall

let it be called what it is

let it be called

# THE SONG OF THE FRIENDS

we call ourselves a family.  in its midst
we walk delicate lines
on the stretched rope of the way
& we are concerned with the right, the moral, & the just.

tho we might consider those terms archaic.
still, we believe in God, & the Lady, in love, & trust
& we are sometimes attacked, from the outside, from the inside, there
        are dangers
so we need to perceive, often, what is right.  what is just.

      one friend painted white lines
      on canvas thru all of one nite
      another smeared over it in the name of love.
      was that right?

we didnt think so.  we dont think so.
but what you do
i can do
what he has done
i have done
yr death is my death, our sickness is one.
so, who's to know?

      another friend came into my house
      & stole precious things. yes he was mad.
      yes he was strung out.
      shd he have done that?

we didnt think so.  we dont think so.
but what you can do
i can do
he has done
what you have done
my death is yr death, our sickness is one.
so who can know?

& there was love.  as a simple fact.
& who can say that it dies, or is born?
i dont know.  probably you dont either.
can the eyes be torn?

we didnt think so.  we dont think so.
but what you do
i do
what you have done, i have done too.
our death & our life & our sickness are one.
we are all concerned with what is just, what is right, what is true.
who's to know?


UNTITLED


belly-wet &
awkward
            grey
gull on the
sand, poking
scurrying

it's hard
work, a daily
grubbing

but suddenly/
activity
            in the air
he flashes

white

serene & timeless
he archs his visionary
path

to a better
place, where there's
something happening, something
belly wet &
grey


## THE ACROBAT


hands & ladder / the act
of balance
the art of the acrobat
who walks
the air
with his fantastic hands
which are not wings

        each step a sweeping somersault, man
        the bones in yr own feet
        shd tell you that

&, as always
no nets


## THE WAVES


they move with the steady rhythm of breath.  they
are the earth's breathings.

they fight each other to bring their exploding
white flowers to the shore.

like tongues & mouths they swallow tensions from
the body, dissolving the self.

they are awesome & hypnotic

it is not that they represent death that they
terrify.

they seem to be a part
of a life so different from mine
that i can only be eyes in their presence

awed eyes.


*UNTITLED*


gull-wing / dancing
the clouds in
the eye of water

gull-cry / grey sky / dull
sun
  grey /
        dancing the sky.
        soft.

has it been said
        birds are souls, flying?

       (is this really what is meant by
            "death"?
       is this sharp clear
       movement
       called
          "dying?"

&.
my feet.  yr feet
so ugly / clumsy
                    like
shapeless,  like
                    frightened.


## JOHN GARFIELD  /  A POLITICAL ELEGY

*For Lack of Time & Thinking, Men Must Love
Each Other Without Knowing Much About it.*

—Camus


1.


1934 1935 ODETS SD ALWAYS ALL
MY LIFE ALL MY EYES WERE BLACK & WHITE
SHOES
          & IT WAS A
PRAYSHRIEK

YOU BEEN THERE JULIE / ME
DIFFERENTLY YES BUT TOO. ME
TOO. PASSED
THRU, MAYBE

EVEN THE SHOES SO
SHINY STILL YR
EYES / LUST LUST


2.


EAST SIDE A DAIRY RESTAURANT YR
JEW MOMS A WAITER SO I KNOW
YOU O YEH JULIE GARFINKLE P.S. 17
          MAYBE /

PARTIAL ROOTS
YR HUNGER VIOLENCE YR DOOMED VISION HOW
YR FACE TWISTED & ALWAYS YR FACE CRYING SOBBING
LIKE A KIDS BURROWED IN THE
MAMA

THE SMASH SHRED GRINDING UNDER
DRIVEN BOOTS FLESH, EYES, VOICE, HUNGER

ALL THE TIME CONJURE YR IMAGE YOU
ARE SWEATING
MOST LIKELY STINK

SMELL ME. I TOO
CRY


*UNTITLED*


we have here
clumsy hands. it is a
joke, how we make
love. as we call it.
as to
the muse /
          she has
her own. a
veritable grace
attendant on
her, flowers
perfumes
&c

*UNTITLED*

charms
totems
formulae of invocation

a shelter.   a safety.

Her concerns differ.  love
must be spoken.
for Her that is my function.
i almost died of power
i almost died of words
almost died of structures
& more, more, any risk
that She use me
to mould the
molten lethal metal

in my hands

i almost died of my hands

SUGGESTED SOLUTION FOR THE PROBLEM
OF UNEMPLOYMENT

no zoo for
put our cages together
label them

it cd be scattered over a
green & open, tho
i dont know who'd picnic on its
sharp sweet smell of
growing uncaged

perhaps cd be opened at special
time
    time for romp
time for playing the i-dont-have-a-cage game
                                    best
stagger the hours or
poets caged by the word
woman caged by cunts
                      (men too this
      section probably be very
crowded)

            kids in cages of
momma daddy all big people

might have huge hate
dances mixed in all together
like people alive mixed up together

some cant be with
any other kind of slave dont want to know
abt being trapped

maybe lots of
architects builders makers of
structure
not functioning good at their wise
hands this might put them at
what they love

a poet has concern for
his community, tho i dont mean
to sound pompous

after all, we
all
live here

# UNTITLED

o patriarchs & jews, clustered round my eyes on the wet beach
dying for thousands of years in flaming self chosen tombs
seeking the Lord
this is the sea from which we all emerged
to try to sing the Lord's tongue to the world
to try to carve our eyes on the wet sand

this is the sea that ultimately will reach
& gulp the burning embers of our screams
& all will be washed & cool
our dying will be wet, & washed, & cooled

washed by the reaching ocean of God's tongue
cooled, rested, chanted in rhythm of the waves

will quiet our wounds
will release our souls from torment
will caress, caress, gently, wavelace tender
& soft, & gathered in, as tho
by love.


## POEM FROM THE CAFE WALL

Lady, you ride the winds that roar
        off the enormous sea & wave
        smashed rocks.
dip, sing, glide, soar,
gull-like, gull-winged, great free
        movement of joy & love & song,
        nothing hidden.
        naked spraying the twisted
human shore
        with beak, claw, wing of your

                    magic gift
            & don't care that
                most pick up not all
                the charged beak/wings of
                        love
            bounce, sing, ride the sun's song,
                            the wind's song.
            back to your hawk-gulled eye.
            no true song dies.
            Lady, my homage & thanks,
                For your gift;
                            my eyes.




                    *UNTITLED*


now i dont have a wife & children any more they live away & they
are making it fine, without
me

& i have the presence of the Muse & the ocean & the woman that i
                            now love
& paint & write & dope up & am totally
irresponsible

beach & shell
bird & wave
woman & brush
books, poets, the long line of great
poems to learn from, how can i
complain?
            & am not, actually.

her hair is long & black
she lets it loose before we
make love & she
is a dancer, moves her whole

body each
kiss

      i think it historically
proper
that she be married & have three kids
of her own
          the Muse has a
funny way of being
funny, who knows what makes Her
laugh?

meanwhile, fucking is real, what it was supposed to be before you
ever did any & my face is re-
shaped & i have a
   new body
when i look in the mirror i see an
unfamiliar person, very lucky
he is
          & she always says: 'why do they say y're so
                         sick?'

because i'm
happy?


## UNTITLED


      everytime you
      answer the door lately
      james cagney bandaged like a mummy
      very dead falls thru

## UNTITLED

recklessly skipping our way in & out of poems
our brains tied together like the threelegged race at
                        the school picnic
not seeing where we are going
only seeing where we are
we are smack pop smashing in a forest of doors
jackboxing up with bebopper surprise
& we have to kaboomzip like fast action rifles
when slam ham screen doors i never closed as a child
all shut at once. suddenly quiet.
we hear the slowing tempo of our marvelous hearts
& we're soared. who's the here? when is the second show?
when dishes popeye yo yo contest matinee ushers
rush down the aisle
stab our ears with chocolate daggers
carved from frozen milky ways.
immobilised. the distant cackle
means that we are trapped
& we can blow give give give & there will be nothing
to give


## UNTITLED


1.


my witch of dark laughter, speaking
moves her hand head gesture finger patterns
as temple dancers guard
devotion's graceful flame

dark my moving witch
laughter of movements
incanting dancing all alive

nakedness of face behind face
intricate the weave
of naked dark alive

bodys of bone & terror
cluster in her warm flowing
they eat her dark laughing
they eat her flesh
they drink her bloods, crack
the bones white in her ebon gesture
hungry they eat drink chew
seeking her sources they suck the shattered splinters sharp

swallowing such razored fragments
lacerates the flesh of throat & gut, releasing
blood, blood, bursting its term channels
flooding the body's interior spaces, filling
until the filled throat strangles

with blood-choked breath they curse her for what they have gobbled of her
in rage they attack the warped
thing their greed has made a grotesque shape
it has no open dark naked
it confronts them, a betrayed thing
they want to kill what they have denied


2.


take care, my darkness
take care, my laughing dancer of every motion
yr witching is precarious gracefulness
a delicate balance, vulnerable
as any human, woman, witch exposed
as live flesh to rot & carrion scavengers

you are yr own being, dark, complete, it fills you with yrself
how good you taste to you
you are for you food, you nourish yr strength

alive with being alive
you are the glittering gem in yr own eye
out of reach of their claws
you are scarred only by yr own visions

o witch of dark lovely
o love of witched laughter
o woman revealed, strong
strong witch, dark
dark, dance, dark
dark my witch, dance
yr laughter
away from their hands of knives
dancing yr whole flesh darkness in laughter witched darkness

blackness of luminous blackness
glowing within you


## UNTITLED


I ONCE KNEW THE WHO
I AM. ALIVE. A HUMAN
ME. NOW NOT KNOWING OBSESSES ME
I DO NOT
AS BIRDS DO / BE
THE CORE.
   THO I HAVE WORDS
FOR IT,
   LIES DO NOT SOAR
HUNGER BLACK & WHITE SCREECH PEACE
BE THAT PURE. THEY CANT

I AM SURROUNDED
BY MY LIFE / IT
WEARING MY FACE, MY
FACE OF PAIN. AN INTERMINGLING.

THE CHILDREN, MY
CHILDREN / THEY ARE
MY HOPE. THEY
HAVE
LOVE. THEY
FORGIVE.


2.


GULLS TREES OCEAN SAND I SEE
ETERNAL. NO LOVE
THERE. LOVE NOT
THERE DESIRED THEIR MOVEMENT
HAS NO ARRIVAL. THEY
MOVE. I MOVE
CRIPPLED ONE WING SHATTERED OR WATER TRAPPED
CLOGGED STRANGLED
                         THO MY
EYES SEE EACH WAVE IMMERSE IN ITS
COMPLETENESS
AT THE SHORE

IT WILL NOT TELL ME
BEING AS IT IS
ITS OWN REAL THING
PERHAPS FOR ME NEVER
WAS MORE THAN WORDS. THE VALUE
OF WHICH
IS WELL KNOWN.

music indiscriminate totality
eats all the push
thrust push lunge of how
each moments live being triggers
fear the animal
cry who i am

in the room
music eats
it eats only power
its own needs
leaves collapsed shattered
fragment timber weathered &
picked over
shaped only how
they touch & hold

it is a clean
place
the music enormous
if not a
the music enormous me in the room
home, a similar
the music enormous me in the room
structure

*22 aug 64*

the street is less real than the sidewalk to a child.

# AN ATTEMPT AT A LETTER A COMMUNICATION

## 1. INVOCATION

o muse, that is not human
speak now as a woman
thru my lips aloud
as you are a god

here i am. yr servant.
as you bend, i am bent. &c
not that i want that changed!
no, if i must be deranged
torn, screaming, insane
i will be. & welcome, too.
what is, is. & comes from you.

there she is. i am here.
between us is all the fear
& hate of ten years,
& all the pain. & the tears.

my voice becomes a whining gibber.
my face is snot & slobber.
she recoils from this face
& its diseased embrace

as she shd. as i do.
as you
o muse
flee that ugly bruise
lady, i pray,
that on this unworthy day
y'll speak, thru my lips, aloud
not that you are human
speak, as you are a god
speak, as you are a woman

## 2. THE LETTER

here, without tears, without death
having made my invocations
hearing no recriminations
filled (perhaps) with the muse's breath

i will try to say.  to see.
something.
            trust the craft ladder down from the tree
trust that the Lady really visits me

what is this need
that you say masks another?
what is the other?
is it a kind of greed?
a last grasp at the mother?

the troubadours say "broken
heart" ( yesm that's that empty feeling
that cannot be spoken.
\          for words are revealing.
for words are concealing.

what do i mean to say?
but this is not the day
i get  to say
all i wanted & meant
to say


## UNTITLED


i know chaos undeniable
where i have never been
total disintegration

i might have
known safety always
might have been denied visions
of flesh & love immensely brite
as rockets random flung to
where i have never been
black as poem—vastness
no, never been
to those limits

hunched, shivered in bone freezing squalls
naked, or clothes in shreds
exposed i remember
where i have never been
unprompted as wind's raging
a place rooted, secure
where i have
warm a place of birth warm of blood
warm a place of bud, warm of flower
where i have warm i
where i have never been


## UNTITLED


my mirror shows a human face.
I see no signs of special grace
deceitfully claimed by my race.
life functions at its rhythmed pace
indifferent to my need for space
where I, & others, may embrace.

## UNTITLED

if i choose to be irresponsible
it does not mean
i am not able to respond
flesh in our world trapped in rooms
packed with traps & people & weapons
responds by recoiling, withdrawing
it attempts to dispatch itself towards a safer reality

even my brain
which must issue the orders
tho perhaps inclined to pursue investigations
unrelated to explosions except in their impact
cannot ignore the alive hand of hate adjusting the piston

not responding can be lethal
involvement equally so
but most dangerous is self delusion
& faith in my limited, deluded, choices


## UNTITLED

nothing of me / needs poems smell
dreams blind with lite
no sacrifice made by me
nor made in my name
moves life but a smidgen, into the lite
that love can descend & warm in her soft bosom
the desperate raging of man's simple hungers
man, once so arrogant, grovels & snivels
he begs, he threatens, he does death skull dances
that he may be granted what none are denied
where is man's warmth, his peace, his devotion?
have they been stolen, that he needs beg for them?

in the streets there is turbulence
men grip the flesh of other men
as tho their hands do not know
it is flesh they clutch.  they
have forgotten human touch
& they rage, rage with cold
they seek warmth in hot blood

all men have the loneliness of their own skins enclosing
but these have gone mad with terror
or else they have sprung
deep from the blooded history of lost ancestors
to be another kind of animal than human, a parasite, a destroyer
eternal changeling, spawn of darkness
devoted to befouling the womb
human it took growth in

that wd explain their fear, & their distance
& why they recoil from love
it is a poison to their poisoned blood

once it was possible to believe man's ultimate flowering
                                        wd be as angel
but now it seems the cancered will devour the living
& no carrion-ghoul, haggard crone, were-cripple, club-back
                                        ever dreamed by man
will be able to match the stench
of the rulers of our future

# FOR MY WIFE'S BIRTHDAY: 13 MAY 66

we celebrate by act
of giving rituals of
offered love

nor as sacrifice
to cleanse the social
the city as organism
a body, stink packed polis barely
held in
contains no holy exchange equal
as sacrament of abasement
begging the gods to eat
what we throw off, throw
up even as responsible communal obligation dedication

shd that not be enuf, all citizens give first pick
of choicest harvests, money
is tithed, human
cock & animal hand
amputated & offered
obedient, hopeful, enormous community faceless

even between man & his gods
the interchange intends to evoke
the taking in of it, & the thing
passed on, beyond,  given
as female Earth, in open, in
ecstasy takes life's joyous flood
takes it all into
Herself encloses

this day is the marked occasion for a giving
life, on a measurably distant day of the same name, itself
was — unpredictably, as life, given

from hand to other
hand, face
to face, love human to
loved human.
it does not evoke, it is itself as
meaning, loving enriched living

the thing given is
as any object not birthed from the flesh is
an object.  hands can hold it, use it
the act of giving, the gift, the interflow
used as a giving into hands of love
to build, to celebrate
revealed by flowers layer by unwreathed on layer
to reveal delicate the center, unashamed
perpetual opening outward, an unfolding, release
as naked as the pulsing flow


## UNTITLED


the collector of words locks himself in his mirror
threatening in falsetto voice
all violence of
lost in the shatter of glass splinter
lost in the dark streets of decay
stumbling & shouting his face masking blindness

what fear heats his blood to flush his flesh fevered
stepping from doorways
stepping into corners

*watch out* !

the warning
spreads his fear along each nerve fiber network
thrum throb thrum

his arms are lumpy with scar tissue & wounds
ancient & recent
blood dried crust scab
blood flowing fresh
smelling his own blood stink

                    quite clearly
it doesnt add up
it isnt meant
*whose* purpose triggers
each gesture of murder or tenderness

                    (which the source secret
          each separate wave
          carries its shattered memory
          long many miles across
          the face
          of the sea)

## UNTITLED

apes have pale skins & hands full of fingers
all pointed identically as they curl around a branch
to swing from, to swing
at sudden appearance of threat

man's thumb brings tension to his hands
flexible, forcing extensions
because it is my hand my hand
no more justified or valuable than the ape's
grabs, grips, crushes, holds
all tools
delicate & dangerous

even while reaching to another, another hand, or body
my human thumbed thing finds it easier
to clutch  / shatter / destruction
& its necessary tools seem always imminent
at the exact moment
the hand unlocks, unfolds, the hand
a flower with its pulse-beat
open to the sun

the hands remember tools/
this demands it close
around one.  it then
functions as the tool insists

it must release
it must gesture, caress, lie open
the touching flesh warm wants no tools
nothing built as structure, rather
a letting go, a looseness, un-
apelike & untooled

to receive tender
the tender hand open as
metal & clubbed stick strike
only the earth


### UNTITLED


a poet told me
in prison he saw
"as close as from here
to there"

          it was in
the black palace
(5 murders in one week)

he sd:
"are you paco?"
       & then
a knife
       (for so many years
       man has sharpened steel
       on his own bone)

the first blow hammered thru the eye to the hilt
the second ripped the roof of the mouth
many blurring hand strokes brite swift blades
punctured paco

a madness, a living in madness
one small incident in the death song clacked by the stones


## A SPECIAL MESSAGE FOR RACHEL

silken hair
face so fair
a magic spell
weaves my Rachel

eye of brite
feet of dance
i wd kiss her
had i the chance!

414

## UNTITLED

the fire burned
burned
burned

& it devours even now
all in its path that is burnable

from such long & intense knowing
of its flaming eyes
we have learned to walk unharmed

naked

open

in its radial center


## FOR MY WIFE ON OUR FOURTH ANNIVERSARY

walls & needs are structured between us
as time marks our flesh & our souls over the distance
in isolate prisons
we can remember celebration
our voices are hoarse with the unheard chanting
with which we pray deliverance
& call each other's names

& darkness is heavy
& distance is heavy
& time continues, flesh heavy
with decay, skin heavy with tears

so how to say love?
how to say it, even
that not being action, life, touching

no words come. love
stays deep, a stone in the gut
a knife, a wound

Unpublished Poems from the 1970s

## UNTITLED

lonely, the beach looks
cold, the water muddy grey
short sharp sullen surf
seems angry, smashing, snorting.
suddenly the sky is filled with gulls
flying round & round in circles within circles with
weightless grace.
circling in opposite directions like a child's thumbs
the breaking!
    moving further down the sky, circling again
barely missing each other
never breaking the pattern
of open exploding flowers strewn thick on the sky

## UNTITLED

*i made my contract with truth*
    —Neruda

  the same one i did?  is there
  a standard form, with blank
  spaces for names
  & statistics?
     it cd as easily be
     each structured
     individually

  mine seemed simple enuf
  (perhaps a little one-sided)
  a matter of total commitment
  & intention.  love, joy, not in
  the terminology

  at this point

in my life
i see clearly
i was cheated

truth never intended to fulfill
contractual obligations

& now
i cant even find
my copy


## UNTITLED


perhaps distance is the same kind of lie
time is a distortion of what is known
to be real
with a structured envelopment.
a confusion

how else to deny
obliteration than by this
touching that we
across unmeasurables
touch.  each other.  known
to be
known to be real.


## UNTITLED


woman
moving thru man, thru the
world.  has her

perpetuity / they call
it mystery
       that man, the
male, cant know
her, how she
is / i mean
myself.  & all others
with cocks know
it so.  it is
a worship.


2.


they make power
of their
unknown to us their
cuntness
       we guess only
its strength & beauty

they know us
our cocks & power
as we know them / a dark
knowing, disasterous
she, blundering, in her way, seeks
the true
image / an
easing

i dont like to see the poem
as vomit
splashing on the upturned faces.
dont prophets develop iron digestions
all those years in the desert?
but swallowing some
things puts the
stomach in an up
roar.
        some swallow, hold
in, the stomach walls
bleed, a sick
bleeding shoots out their
cocks into their wombs
& the women are impregnated
with foul blood.  & the children
are born, foul & sick, sick
blood, sick
bleeding in their veins.

the moon pulls blood
from the women, rhythm
of life, & they
hide it, are
shamed & secret.  destroy.

but blood, vomit, shit, flowers
stream forth from the
mouth, red
brite life &
excretion
puked over the
fleeing
creatures.
        o my fellow
           citizens!
y're not expected to taste

it, bathe in
it, surging waves of
horror.  run.  run from the
rotting rutting
stench, the sticky, almost sweet
clinging.  it is hard
to stand still.  i know.  i, too
dont like to see the poem
as vomit, the poem as
blood.  the poem as
wound.


*UNTITLED*


here is the poet (myself) in madness
not screaming
not plunging blind embracing
dangerous magics

is it the weight of time contains the rhythms
to structures ration in form, & bearing
labels of stability?
or is the seemingly verified
sanity itself
another image of
deluded desperation?
each level
demands its own answer

meanwhile:  clocks
tick, the body moves in its fat rhythms
functioning by its total
knowledge i cannot share

## UNTITLED

by way of the ear, brains are shattered.  even the most
accurate maps have large blank spaces boundaried by fear & con-
taining nothingness.  a utopia of despair.

growth distorts form.  crushed against each other, we viciously
guard our pockets.  the pollen rejects the bee.  the hanged man shits
squirts semen.  citizens maintain the structures.

the assault is constant, perhaps the tree outlives its pain.  or
the rock face of the earth Herself.  a politics of distance.

## UNTITLED

there are judges judging.  their
totem image is blindfolded
this keeps her pure, her sight
undefiled

strange are the uniforms
man wears for his dances.  how intricate
the movements & gestures
by which he relates to himself

this house in which we live
is not my father's house
tho there are many rooms
dark & hidden passages
obscure & frightening
at the table where the maps & scripts are sold
all is confusion & shouting voices
pages are not numbered
selection is totally haphazard
there are no reliable instructions

perhaps it has always been like this
scholars of history
cannot agree

"living" camus sd
                              "naturally
is never easy"

did he have to say "naturally"?


## UNTITLED


please take yr posts at the weapons-racks!
we'll see what good all yr training has been
i see everything is polished
i see the pits of satisfactory depth & blackness
for the corpses

exercise number 5: all together!
one! clutch! two! press! three! withdraw!
                                        excellent!

flesh teams to the fore!
sensitivity destructors advance!
mirror shatterers! skin deceivers! corpse factions!
be prepared to call the amount
of sexual disintegration
in geometric progression!

now begin removal of all faceless compassion
the self deceivers are instructed to report to headquarters

425

again to the weapons racks!  seize! fire! destroy!
replace the weapons & resume positions
ultimately all preparations
will be undertaken
in which each has his place
& each place is filled


## UNTITLED


go to the huge prison
go to the cement cities
go to the desolate fields of war
go to the echoing chambers of government
go to the buildings in which our children are chained
you will find all there
the executioner as well as the torn & shattered flesh
know the word
                    love

which means
that words cannot save us
what it means abt love
i do not know
nor the meanings that flower into angels of flame
as images fall from my eyes like dust
& all is unbreathable & poisoned
how can i call down destruction upon the race
or even the society in which i feebly function?
terror strikes me
i do not want the lightning of the gods to burn my brain
I too am a coward
(even as you are, brother,
even as you)

## POEM AGAINST THE PRESIDENT, UPON HIS INTENSIFICATION OF THE SLAUGHTER

i must look
into myself
to find
such a monster


## UNTITLED

i have been accused
of imagery grim with reality

poems of fear & awareness of man's integral blackness
undeniably bear
my signature

considering this indictment
i called forth my images
to be precisely identified, committed

a brilliant precision!  flashing! turning! dancing! a dance
intended only to praise
& illuminate
that which is

even the dim & destructive
patterns twisted trapped our eyes our screams
are exalted & transformed
by the reality of their being

UNTITLED

hubris malignant runs mad as man
unable to shape & control
destroys
destroys all
destroys all he    touches, even
especially
himself poisoning his food
strangling on human vomit in his lungs
his machines & his bones

interchangeable
rotted & immutable

there is no rest
when flesh will not return to earth
but will lay, alien
midst layers of unreal garbage, man's chemical
vision / permanent
in terms of human chronology

eventually the entire universe
(perhaps) will return
to chaos, its origin
man, then, also, his flesh, his poems
will go under, into, become
part of it, the whole
process / but for now
we eat
we breathe
we shape our hopes & visions, our gods
within rhythms overwhelmingly
terrifying

*UNTITLED*

all wander the signless streets
a search for surety & direction
on pages no names can be read
instruments of communication are silent & dark

with the aid of his thumb man discovered tools
out of that brief moment of wonder & power
this grotesque world has
been shaped / a design
proliferating upon itself like maddened death within the flesh
death eating life, eating death, eating meaning
memory a weapon in the war of mirrors
treacherous & elusive, but recognisable as to its language

within the massive groupings
indistinguishable faces turn one to the other
i turn toward you, you seek another, each reaches, moves
                              tries to breathe & flow
if asked, unanswered
if sought, unseen
if touched, unfeeling
if known, distorted

man, a memory, a weapon of mirrors
frozen to his tools of bewilderment & fear

*UNTITLED*

women walk
past my window. i
as by command of this
flesh, these breasts, haunches, this
physical shell, give

joyous attention
reverence, even.  it is not only
lust, tho
lust is present
        (i pray the Lady it not offend)
       but more, more
             i am

a man
a poet
recipient of the Lady's
curse/blessing
        always seeking

Her
She who
rides wildly the individual human
female
rides the flesh, the soul, the very
earth from which it all
thrusts
past my window
in & out of my life

myself
at best, poet
observer
recorder of rituals & worship

how can we
meet?
touch?
touch real?

## UNTITLED

i see gardens of disasters being carefully cultivated
altho the young move freely within the joy of their bodies
it appears they, too, are doomed to drink
the deadly concoction of toenails
distilled from the poems of corpses

do you, my leaders & instructors
deny my visions of injectable traumas?
flowers! flowers! screaming for the scientists' machined calibrations
stain as with blood the bridal cassandras
untouchable, virgin, illuminated by death

in the midst of my eyes, how is it the dance
still ecstatic! bewildering! chaotic!
maintains its massive rhythms of celebration?


## HOW I AM: A LETTER TO JOAN THORNTON

i am a mass of weighted flesh, hungering
i am blindness, seeking lite
i am confused by the colors of the days
i am weeping joyously
i am in pain, but i am dancing, clumsily, but rhythmically

in my external aspects the movements seem sure & unhesitant
the eyes are brite & laughter raucous
but all the time terrible machines are calculating within
                              my skull
disrupting the patterns, feeding in new evaluations, new
                              information
predictions shatter
pinwheels of imperatives! fragmented mirrors blinding in
their imagery! chaos! movement! hunger!

431

my bone-deep fear of heights
has not yet thrust me screaming
from this balanced perch
tho terror leers, prods, waits
knowing me for what i am

thru it all, it is the hunger that searches
not only for satisfaction, but to satisfy
feed me by my feeding you
it says
but there is little response

perhaps "feed me by my feeding you"
is frightening
perhaps it is devious, a trick, a manipulation
i may not be real, nor you, nor anything that might pass
                    between us or between anyone
but to me i am
that is how i am
i am all this & more
these are only words & i am only a man

& you.  how are you?
how are you?




BEN TALBERT
*"this the face of god . . ."*


a man who worships flesh &
art.  tho thru his art
transforms the flesh, reinvents the actual
fucking!  impossible?  yes, impossible
as even life, as, certainly
love, is
            impossible.
                        ben

talbert.  they told me
he was dying.  as he is.  as
we all are

                but as he dies, as he
lives, his trembling hand
brings brush to image
again & again & again
making multidimensioned the simple
lusts & purities of
mouth over cock, prick in cunt
bodies writhing in gentle rhythms
against each other in a world of exploded
fear & desire
                        paintings.  as man has done
since he transcribed on walls of solid rock
his dances & his totems & his dreams
painting with the reality of vision
with the vision of flesh
flesh transformed by touch of flesh
flesh transformed by touch of hand
the hand of the man who so
paints the flesh against the flesh

beyond the rigid categories of the mind
including everything thought & hoped for
more than even secret hungers can invent
his eye & hand exalt the physical being
man & woman & woman & woman
as his love is for the touching
as his hand is for the transcription of the miracle
as his miracle is for the exaltation of
his hands
his eyes
his undeviating total demand of uncorrupted
human angel
dangerous visions of
flesh to flesh in our world of pain

# THE TWO PAINTERS
### *for Don Martin*

soutine in a dark room
thick paint stink filth
the lite / its sadness
its own weight

      slept on a bed his

uprooted flesh surrounded by
steel enamel wood water
holders intended as
impregnable to cockroaches & vermin
on every surface encrusted their constant hunger
movement undulating the walls
& the world / deceptive lite off
their brittle black shells blindly
shifting glints & shadows making
a huge horror funhouse mirror eye-twisting to his hurt vision

wise creatures, magicians of their race
with the skill of centuries drink
the water fortress
to make safe crossing for their
hordes.  soutine twitching & alive with eyes
weeping paint stink & color hunger his tears
perpetual, refilling.  perhaps
an act or gesture
of hope, or memory

      while on the floor
on & in the steady migration insect flow
over his face & hands picking from his eyes & lustful flesh
some measure of salt or nourishment
modigliani slept / a pretty italian
woke / a pretty italian
scraped the walls' living skin clean enuf
to paint without acknowledging his roach-filled mouth
his slender hungers of faces

their world filled with its own clean lite
breasts no dark & ancient creature walked

soutine's eyes were dark red & heavy black
soutine's eyes swallowed lite & spit out gloom luminous
with tears & brite beetle-glints

the two dancers, eating
each other, still ravenous in the
room  /  the soutine room dark insect
clustered jewesses voluptuous dying in the cockroach lite
the other's room shimmer walls of morphine grace
a tongue-touched flesh, kissable mouths


2.

modigliani died young, always the
southern romantic where warm
the water & sun demanded such a
conclusion.  to make the completion
a kind of compositional balance
painters dream from life his woman leaped
to death to follow him.

                              in his room, unknown
even to himself, gorged on jewish horrors
& loneliness, soutine, exhausted by battle
pushing fist fulls of roaches breaking
teeth tongue cut into his mouth the blood
a vomit of strength & need
covering canvas & mocking lite

alone with his pain, along
with his walls of despised paints & ancient enemies
his despair a frenzy of bottomless desire
gullet stuffed with crawling things
cracking snap wire legs bellys bursting into
his once human flesh
trained now to new foods, drawing life & movement

from the empty shells unblinking eyes
jamming their ceaseless hunger into his ceaseless hunger
until his flesh, black
as the meat it encompassed
stretched, swelled, ballooned
knocking over the bed, the work
table, crushing against the walls
the unused pots & pans as fast as eyes
bleed screams his arms
frenzied grabbing stuffing forgetting to
swallow or chew cockroaches
millions who travelled from russia to paris
to be devoured by soutine the growing filth
devourer millions millions into him in maniac terror
until, roach-filled soutine
in a dark room full
burst undigested insects, paints, fears
splattering smears of soutine
voluptuous, tormented, the hideous
human beauty of his unspeakable hunger
stilled.  permanent on the flesh
fragments framed & forgotten, covered with moving bodies
of insect hunger sharp mirrored
in the dark of the room


*UNTITLED*


november comes to a close
"november, month of martyrs" jackson mac low
called it.  & sounded their names, the
great ones who had gone, under this moon.
now ezra pound's name can be added
to that list
                    (tho i doubt he wd want
to share honors with all those wobblies
& bombthrowers)

also it's the month my wife
& one of my daughters
were born
always i think of this entrance into winter
as grey, grey
but where i am the world is yet
green & golden
                    tho winter breathes its imminent
presence
at the full moon there was poetry
& madness
& rage
despair threatens always to take over
but life struggles towards its joy


## ON PABLO NERUDA'S WINNING THE NOBEL PRIZE


they found him at an embassy, serving
his government.  i wd like to think
the foundations of the building
mined with his words
ready to explode, expand, make clean
the space the State occupies


        (perhaps some rubble
        fragments left to be broken up, carted off
        dumped or melted down
        for use in some structure of joy
        or redemption)

but that, like so much which can be formed
in words, seems romantic
as much a relic of an earlier time
as the source of the prize
given him.  neither dynamite

nor poems
carry the images of power
& cleansing
they once did


## ALBA


we make our garden our own nite heads

& the birds that sing there sing between our bodies

the only watcher against the impending world

stands guard inside our moving limbs

    the nite is wild

    & has a swinging beat

      the moon hides

      & day begins


o lantern held blinding by hands of ominous power

o shining on our movements, shining on our love, shining

                    shining

tear yr eyes from our loveliness, don't make us aware of time

stand on the other rim

for a while

but the nite is wild

& has a swinging beat

the moon hides

& day begins

it brings knives to sever us

it brings clocks to time us

it brings papers for us to sign

it brings us

others


so, my love, we must tear down all the roses in the garden

& crush the song from the throats of the soft birds

in yr breasts

& attend the watcher who locks & unlocks thighs

for he tells us again

that the nite has been wild

but its beat swings far out

the moon has hidden

& the day has begun

# POEM FOR PHILOMENE

Philomene—
I had a flash/image
of you standing in
what I call yr "nun's
position"—hands clasped,
head bowed, body a
straight line balanced—
& looking at you standing
that way in my
mind—stunned by
the beauty of you—
I realized you look like Maud Gonne—
the Angel of the
Irish Revolution,
Yeats' lifelong
passion & muse
figure—

Philomene—
daughter of lite
bring yr luminous dance
to open new visions
within the black
against which
all struggle

## *UNTITLED*

thru all my life there has been war
born in 1930, i have early memories
of books burning in a mountain of flame defying the nite
of chinese dead sprawled haphazard chaotic on eisenstein steps
bubble gum cards carried pictures of massacres

in spain
in china
the ethiopians flowering into death
( we flipped them against the schoolhouse wall
   winning & losing air-raids & bodies, gas attacks & tortured
                                   victims

slaughter
blood
bones broken & flesh smashed
man extending himself
reaching for the monstrous
destroying destroying destroying
all categories & faces
all races & sizes
killing everything human, the enemy, the others, himself
bringing to this task
his technological brilliance
his uncharted psyche
his distorted visions

i say "man", i say "his"
what "man" does, i do, you do
        *even if we dont know how*
war / death / destruction / pain


2.

i remember clearly
the process of structure
my mind's shaping
what seems to me real

a vision expanding
man's growth into angel
all holiness present
life as divinity

this vision has been purified
by many journies
thru my own blackness
& depths of being


3.

but how, i wonder, to seek joy
as even now i close myself off for protection
when my own openness leads in only to more doors, unopened
when so much that is love i know only as memory, at a distance
what can i expect of any, of our world, of myself?
yet, even as my pen makes lists of disasters
& my eyes are filled with my own faults & failures
still, my being quickens to the name of love
still, the images of freedom & joy call forth my tears &
                                                    desires
i remain, this day, 12, october 1972
holy
imminent
human


## WHY I AM NOT WRITING POEMS AGAINST
## THE VIET-NAM WAR


it is the war within catches my energies
life is so brief all perception is
timeless, frozen in the vastness of all realities
realities indifferent to pain, to love
to all things human

all our history does not make
a visible gesture
across the infinite stage

or, i may be only trying
to justify how i feel
cut off from the world, as tho
it all takes place, not superficially
but on some other surface

which i can only view
in two dimensions

the drive to contact, to resolution
is obsessive
                altho, part of me doubts
even that achievement
wd satisfy
wd breach, wd
bridge

another part
& another
& others, others
parts, segments, facets, movements, rhythms
each insisting upon its own
reality

the war within
which has trapped my energies


ODE TO SHEEP


the sheep
eat.  move
on.  eat.  lie
down.  rise.  move
again.  eat
more.  small ones
following, their

spasmed movements
seeming
joyous. eat. move. eat.
their lives are
quiet &

uncomplex among
the hills
of infinite variations
of green & yellow
of red & brown
of colors as yet
unnamed &
unknown surrounding
ancient altars
of erupted rock
which once burst
screaming thru
the skin
of the earth
but now are
silent, massive
in the total
rhythm of
completeness.

it is not
wise to read
such images
in human terms.
what i feel, so
fulfilled
protected
part of
surrounded by
it & them
may not be
what they
eating, resting
eating, moving

in this
earth solid
stillness
know as
bone & flesh
of love's
nourishment.


## THE GREAT AMERICAN EXPERIMENT
## AMERICAN KNOWHOW & ALL THAT ROT

the crunch in yr gut
when u know
u got nuthin to say
abt not wanting to know
all that:  a chair is the blues shit

a building in left field
can be considered as a natural object
a japanese saw
a child's absurd faith in the way
things get done

spare a word
wordman
sumone hit the target number
even the simplest clues are denied me
a horse in the nest
my tongue in my shoe
& everytime i say beer i push a muscle
an incredible absence
every body's being careful
a tape in the hand & a pocket & a whip
i make decisions weakwilled
nostrils clogged w/menthol

face full of fastlaffs
put my life in a hefty bag

convince yrself
throw that overhand curve

of all the best
of the ones i luv
talking talking
rolling along mutely
not one image:
how cd such smiling men be conned

we've always been involved w/the currency flow
we put our money back in the system
we are not hoarders


so:  the dept of punitive people
offered me a guest shot
& i failed in my mission
i hit the target
but did not score

there are 3 or 4 instances
in each day
when 7000 motorized lawnmowers
an unlimited supply of nervous elbows
& a fleming jug & bottle cutter
challenge the cribbage champion of north america

these are political times.
the streets are jammed, tension mounts.
groups form, armed, ready to pounce
on perpetrators of civil crimes.

the leaders are denied
yet they lead.  upright
citizens, heads tight
assuage their fears with pride.

language is betrayed.
meaning has been stolen
from words.  faces are swollen
with lies, delusions parade.

the holders of power, inflamed
with hunger for more, more power
bring to sinister flower
the movements of their game.

the glacial weight of history
crushes with massive pressure.
man, who shd be the measure,
finds his world a mystery.

the politics are obscure.
the future is not known.
the roads have not been shown.
the visions are not pure.


### UNTITLED


reaching a place of
resting, now i find me
thinking of he
from whom i ran / my
face, man touching
other man, foully
as tho i cant leave it
be, picking at it like
a broken finger nail y're
not going to rip or clip
but see how long it can be
let hang there, &
played with

fortunately, i am
mad, & in a foreign
country / keeps me
to myself

there is no real resting, the
heart, the lungs, they're
working


## UNTITLED


cold winds clear the streets of pleasure seekers
only the most serious remain in view
the followers of words, the dancers
voluptuous, mysterious, filled with images of ecstasy & death

dilettantes of life survive the winter
using all technologies of protection
walls behind walls in front of deceptions
labyrinths of avoidance filled with optimists

other rhythms (more natural, perhaps
exhaust themselves & us
chilled by the winds boned external

## THE ANGRY MAN ON THE MOUNTAIN
*for James Ryan Morris*


why does he scream?
why does he cry?
so that his tears will blur the edges
of his visions
of the loss of love


## FOR BRENDA


flesh angel
here you encompass
take in & nourish
me.  here, in a strange city
of flux & significance
you, a miracle of being
of being alive

many poets chronicle the perfect breasts & gestures
which She repeats thru the history of flesh
to exalt & humble
men & poets

but no mention is made of
that you are a lite which
not only illumines but transforms
you bring flowers out of the nite
& i, too, in my flesh & my eyes
feel the surge of the new buds
thrusting towards the lite
you make solid & holy in yr
vibrant
                physical abundance

2.

i talk of yr flesh because that is what i touch, what touches me
but more than flesh is mingled when we enter each other
there are no words
there are too many words
for all that is exchanged
in the hot wetness
of all the openings drinking each other


# IN POUND'S LAST YEARS IN VENICE, ITALY


they came as pilgrims to his aging
in the city of water where overlooked the flow
past his window & his mind

they came to receive words
they hoped for poems
they wanted to wrap their emptiness
in his still growing structures
to receive the brand of his tongue on their flesh & their needs

& they got silence from him
& they got querulousness & ancient midwestern cackled slang
or they got only the nothing
they brought with them

because they cd not overhear
as he & henry james talked, not of history, or money
but of the garbage in the canals
of the city they both so loved

how can i sing, speak, chant, or even make
coherent in my own eyes
the visions i hear fragments of?

the words i am given
are old, have lived too long
in mouths of lies & death.  they
barely remember
meanings once contained.

i want to see it, say it, whole
instead, images flash by, dazzling my brain
with explosions of human reaching & need
into a universal poem

uni = single
verse = song
one song all sings.  the world above
is ruled by the world below
man & the source locked, a marriage, as of one flesh

that much is clear.  but that is clearly
not enuf.  nor does it satisfy
to know that what is sought is
unutterable.  perhaps
unknowable.
                    still, the hunger drives
on, carrying me with it
into it, consumed & consuming
a cold fire, it does not burn
but illuminates

earth is not ageless, but it is old, old
more ancient than can be chanted
within boundaries of what man calls knowing
cities & gods are not returned to rubble
becoming mountains of memory
weaving from air & destruction
a veil of masks & gems, a shroud obscuring
even the funeral dances
which celebrate the passing
no one knows how many cycles have been completed
but the sea's rhythm is a clue to how time was
before it was measured, as it flowed freely, denying days & ages
it is sd there were giants on earth
& in the hearts of men
all knowledge was pure
divinity part of the animal acts of living
man eating & dying as the structure of temples
building, reaching, rising to awakenings of spirit
cycle after unknown cycle has been covered by soil & jungle
only to begin again with all knowledge lost, wiped clean, forgotten
digging crudely into caves which conceal the unreadable secrets
with everything to be reinvented, even man himself
who had achieved the piercing of the veils of esoterica
once again finding his hand a stranger to the tools he discovered
                                   fragmented in the rocks
to break a stone upon a stone a matter of revelation & miracle
to again emerge, find others
family expanding to include group
group becoming tribe
the process culminating
in complex organic relationships, community
man knowing man, with his eyes on the ever awesome universe
until, as the wave falls to the sand
the rhythm of man's culture curves downward, disintegrates
again & again, uncountable times, unknowable time
returning to the source, emerging again, returning
the point of beginning is not known

nor direction
                    (if those are not the same thing, without the restric-
                    tions of counting & measurement
unmeasureable, old, going back & moving forward
maybe it will be possible
someday to reach some resolution
other than the conquering jungle
& the oblivion of forgetfulness




## UNTITLED


i went to hear kirby doyle read
it was at ucla a maze of glass mountains
jack hirschman showed me a book of hebrew letters
kabbalah! poems! madness!
this was years ago

not long after that i went to prison
a desert of concrete & steel sterility
the i ching told me to perservere
& i thot of the hebrew book
& the doyle poems abt
dope! motorcycles! john garfield! love!
that, too, now, is in
the past
in the present i am surrounded by books
                    (the past)
heading towards the future (the past)
slowly
too fast
instantaneously NOW becomes
it is still the present
all in the past

as everything is
or will be

## UNTITLED

i send spies into the territory
of myself. those who return
(all do not return)
are changed beyond recognition
they are infected with anxieties & fantasies
locked in, bent over, whispering
behind their hands
secretive beyond furtiveness

in the war to outwit my own sterility
i want poems to fall from my hands to the page
from my eye to yr eye
fall, fly, soar, wing thru
my space, yr space, the space
we share & that which is
distance.     leaped by the
poem, a bravado, a falling, falling
into the light
bringing the light with it
a wholeness
a reverence
a healing

you say we are together in this house
by accident of circumstance & love
to satisfy simple needs with what consideration
we can bring to the acts of living

"accident" is a word describing
how fragments fall together
when the pattern is not known, but knowing
we are moved by, flowed thru, carried along

we watch & we listen.  i listen
to you, not because i love you
but for the greediest of reasons:  what
i learn as you fill my ears, my eyes, my
whole head & being
with what you know, see, do.  you
present yrself as you are, totally
a purity of vision

as in a poem, all is clarity
with many levels seeming obscure
how can it be
i learn abt myself & how i love
from how you touch the plants?
if i am asked abt god
i wd have to tell how by yr example
i know abt love which does not hold or obligate

as in a poem
there are times you talk
& i don't know the words, how they relate.  then
later i am illuminated

you teach me to be me
by being you.  we are together
for this part of the journey
i know my back is covered

i gladly call you brother
i state unambiguously that
divinity pours thru you
even tho i never saw
the lite from yr eyes extending over the street
i have seen you reaching out towards
something hurt & needing, with such love
i cd have walked upon it.  i know you make no claims, & i
can only report what i know to be true.  i know
whatever of my life has been shared
with you has been enriched.  the rituals
we have danced thru
have been performed joyously, out of deep need

you emerged from the sea & stood hugely tall & glowing
making a binding, a wholeness
to teach me abt love.  you came to me
in prison, to teach
me abt love.  not that you are
didactic, it's just how you move
thru what is demanded of you
with such grace & awe, feeling
that sweet-tinged fear
of presumptuousness on the edge of the abyss
                                        no matter
how dark & ominous, you will descend.  if
you can mark a path for
me, & others, you will
but, path or not, i walk gladly into darkness with you
if we emerge into lite, we will be thankful
if the black suffocation is eternal, we wont be surprised
hand in hand with you
          (for we know how to touch
           in lite or gloom)
i wd sing praises echoing thru the labyrinths
resounding with yr name & the names we reverence
always i wd sing, there wd be no despair
by one of many roads we will find what we seek

# UNTITLED

let me take my city into my wounds
slashed by lumined jewels of sand
that glow & sting their songs & wings
into our flesh made soft by blood & rot & lice

let me take my city into my hand
my flesh-whipped, fluttering hand, not gull
not even claw of flight
to hold as close as winds under the enveloping wing

let me ride the wing of wind that sings
the erupted earth into the air
the still wing, pierced, trembling
that climbs from slab to slab of stone step, sky

feed my city to me in the fresh
explosion of our joyous flesh
flying my city to my eternal touch
as we, & it, sing the gull triumph
of our rage
& our joy

# DEAREST PHILOMENE

All energies recirculate

Unity is affirmed

Singularity is

    divinity—

    love,

    Stuart

## *UNTITLED*

cities are destroyed
much the same as in
days of bronze & stone
different gods called upon
other flags

the massive destructive groupings
have long been recognised
from great distances their symmetrical pulse
alerts the future victims

all men are brothers
but brothers are capable of all, all

that we are here
& others, also, live in our eyes
makes hope continuous
in the face of history's warnings

perhaps what is heard is not
the cadenced feet of men
with faces cold, wet with sweat
erupting from infection within
but rather
the first great throb
of wings preparing to lift
the entire race
to carry it
aloft, above, beyond
what has been hinted


## POEM FOR A SPECIAL OCCASION


in the inescapable cities
thru which we run
crouched against cold winds
seeking a way
out, a way
thru, come tunnel or doorway
of warmth or direction
a man knows his brothers
by the blood they share

many dark passages
can only be travelled
single file, each being
extension of each, till all
arrive, safely

when naked crawling endless wastes of ice & history
only the close flesh warmth
of others, crawled together, gathered
will protect

no telling what millions wd starve
if hands not their own
did not lift the bread

how is it done?  a meeting
a sharing of inadequate strengths
till all
are stronger, a touching
then
a moving on, towards
another hoped for
joining


## FOR ALEXANDER SOLZHENITSYN

& you
not even a jew
as the hand of power reaches
to crush yr flesh & vision

marching up to the very edge, then going further in their vehicles which crawl
    the earth's skin
digging deep & discarding everything, bone, bottle, verse, equally condemned
in their terrored flight
as birds wing to their deaths uncomplaining in the nite air over them
they cannot forget you
they have torn you from yr rooted joy & wrapped you in their steel gaunted
    holsters
shrouding yr presence as a wound is wrapped & hidden
seeking yr obliteration under their huge wheels

a long road back you must travel
a journey of return
to the kingdom of nite, enslaved
not only by yr enemies
but by the face you will remember from having worn it
before.  it does not change

it is a command stronger than fear
She puts on yr tongue
yr protests will not help,  She needs
yr pain and clarity
for Her own purposes

traveling mapless by instinct & memory
you will move thru the dark tunnels
the lite which pulses from the core of yr being
human will barely
illuminate.  each step a risk.  but you
having once emerged from the abyss
know a way can be found
without markings or definitions
what choice have you?  none.  & none
to help or guide.  only what you know
is real
including those trapped by their distorted masks who strangle yr cries
can protect you now

no one can walk with you
where many have walked
with yr same pride
& terror

## UNTITLED
*[handwritten poem, taken off Stuart's wall 6/27/74]*


so black, The visions.  That's why they
linked gaunted arms & stumbled towards
the flames in a feeble dance of celeb-
rations.  For the visions cannot be
denied, reality is irrevocable &
so, precisely *there* they found joy
& song.

      Grant me that strength
he who must remain
unnamed


*Stuart Z. Perkoff (July 29, 1930 - June 25, 1974)*